Fast C ~~D0287259~~

The Young Adult's Guide to

Pet Sitting & Walking

Yvonne Bertovich

FAST CASH: THE YOUNG ADULT'S GUIDE TO PET SITTING AND WALKING

Copyright © 2017 Atlantic Publishing Group, Inc.

1405 SW 6th Avenue • Ocala, Florida 34471 • Phone 800-814-1132 • Fax 352-622-1875
Website: www.atlantic-pub.com • Email: sales@atlantic-pub.com
SAN Number: 268-1250

No part of this publication may be reproduced, stored in a retrieval system, or transmitted in any form or by any means, electronic, mechanical, photocopying, recording, scanning, or otherwise, except as permitted under Section 107 or 108 of the 1976 United States Copyright Act, without the prior written permission of the Publisher. Requests to the Publisher for permission should be sent to Atlantic Publishing Group, Inc., 1405 SW 6th Avenue, Ocala, Florida 34471.

Library of Congress Cataloging-in-Publication Data

Names: Bertovich, Yvonne, 1995- author. | Atlantic Publishing Group, issuing body.
Title: Fast cash : the young adult's guide to pet sitting and walking / by Yvonne Bertovich.
Description: Ocala, Florida : Atlantic Publishing Group, Inc., [2017] | Includes bibliographical references and index.
Identifiers: LCCN 2017022581| ISBN 9781620231678 | ISBN 1620231670 | ISBN 9781620231685 (ebook)
Subjects: LCSH: Pet sitting—Vocational guidance—Juvenile literature. | Dog walking—Vocational guidance—Juvenile literature.
Classification: LCC SF414.34 .B47 2017 | DDC 636.088/7—dc23
LC record available at https://lccn.loc.gov/2017022581

LIMIT OF LIABILITY/DISCLAIMER OF WARRANTY: The publisher and the author make no representations or warranties with respect to the accuracy or completeness of the contents of this work and specifically disclaim all warranties, including without limitation warranties of fitness for a particular purpose. No warranty may be created or extended by sales or promotional materials. The advice and strategies contained herein may not be suitable for every situation. This work is sold with the understanding that the publisher is not engaged in rendering legal, accounting, or other professional services. If professional assistance is required, the services of a competent professional should be sought. Neither the publisher nor the author shall be liable for damages arising herefrom. The fact that an organization or Web site is referred to in this work as a citation and/or a potential source of further information does not mean that the author or the publisher endorses the information the organization or Web site may provide or recommendations it may make. Further, readers should be aware that Internet Web sites listed in this work may have changed or disappeared between when this work was written and when it is read.

TRADEMARK DISCLAIMER: All trademarks, trade names, or logos mentioned or used are the property of their respective owners and are used only to directly describe the products being provided. Every effort has been made to properly capitalize, punctuate, identify, and attribute trademarks and trade names to their respective owners, including the use of * and ™ wherever possible and practical. Atlantic Publishing Group, Inc. is not a partner, affiliate, or licensee with the holders of said trademarks.

Printed in the United States

PROJECT MANAGER: Danielle Lieneman
INTERIOR LAYOUT AND JACKET DESIGN: Nicole Sturk

Reduce. Reuse.
RECYCLE.

A decade ago, Atlantic Publishing signed the Green Press Initiative. These guidelines promote environmentally friendly practices, such as using recycled stock and vegetable-based inks, avoiding waste, choosing energy-efficient resources, and promoting a no-pulping policy. We now use 100-percent recycled stock on all our books. The results: in one year, switching to post-consumer recycled stock saved 24 mature trees, 5,000 gallons of water, the equivalent of the total energy used for one home in a year, and the equivalent of the greenhouse gases from one car driven for a year.

Over the years, we have adopted a number of dogs from rescues and shelters. First there was Bear and after he passed, Ginger and Scout. Now, we have Kira, another rescue. They have brought immense joy and love not just into our lives, but into the lives of all who met them.

We want you to know a portion of the profits of this book will be donated in Bear, Ginger and Scout's memory to local animal shelters, parks, conservation organizations, and other individuals and nonprofit organizations in need of assistance.

— Douglas & Sherri Brown,
President & Vice-President of Atlantic Publishing

Table of Contents

Introduction...9

Chapter 1: Basics of Pet-Sitting................................... 13

Do You Have What It Takes? 13

Common Job Duties... 19

Types of pet-sitters and possible services................ 22

Gaining Experience 25

Chapter 2: Becoming the World's Best Boss 29

Business Plan 29

Naming and brand development................................ 30

Outlining your plan...33

Business summary...34

Management summary.. 35

Products and services 36

Check out the competition......................................36

Service area 36

Strategy for services 37

Marketing and social media 38

Budgeting 39

Initial and operational expenses 39

Transportation costs 39

Adding up your worth 40

According to my calculations 41

Payment policies 45

Some Quick Business Do's And Don'ts 48

Client Agreements 51

Sample Client Agreement 52

Sample Pet Information Form 53

Chapter 3: Caring for Your Clients 57

Meeting New Clients 57

Conducting a client interview 58

Visiting Procedures 62

Visit Checklist 63

What's in a service kit? 64

Basic Types of Care 65

Dogs 65

Cats 67

Hamsters, Gerbils, and more 70

Fish 71

Amphibians 72

Snakes, turtles, and other reptiles 73

Birds 74

Other 74

Maintaining Relationships 76

Making your clients feel special 80

Quality control 81

Business Policies *82*

Sample Client Checklist.......................................*84*

Sample Veterinarian Notification....................*86*

Following up *86*

Dealing With Difficult Clients..........................**87**

Pesky pets..*87*

Pesky people *89*

Keeping Safety in Mind......................................**90**

What to do in emergency situations *90*

Chapter 4: Spreading the Word............... 93

Advertising Tips **93**

Printed ads and fliers...*95*

Digital ads and more..*97*

Cold calling..*97*

Social Media...**97**

Facebook *99*

Twitter...*99*

Instagram *99*

WordPress or website resources *101*

Other social media sites to consider............*102*

Email Marketing..**102**

*How exactly can I get into email
marketing?* *103*

What should I be emailing my clients?.......*103*

Chapter 5: Expanding Your Business 107

How to Track Your Success **107**

Keeping records...*108*

How to Know if You're Ready for More 108

   Where do you even begin?...*108*

Possible Expansion Ideas...111

   Pet grooming..*111*

   Pet products...*112*

   Pet bakery *113*

Keeping You and Your Business Thriving...................115

   How to avoid burnout *115*

   Building a foundation for the future........................*117*

Conclusion 119

Bibliography..121

Glossary 123

Appendix...129

Sample Client Checklist................................. 129

Sample Veterinarian Notification..........................131

Sample Business Plan Outline 131

Sample Business Plan: Reganne Yorkie's
Pet-Sitting Service 132

Pet Grooming Resources.................................. 138

Index 141

About the Author...143

Introduction

For some human beings, it's difficult to even wake themselves up every day and make sure that they're properly fed, bathed, and clothed. They think they should receive a medal each time they remember to drink a glass of water, brush their hair, or wear non-stretchy pants.

Now shout-out to the pet-sitters and pet-lovers of the world—you guys tirelessly take care of other living things for little in return. A quick shout-out to those, too, who want to join the ranks of pet-sitters in various levels around the U.S. and world—you've come to the right place. Whether you're entertaining the thought of starting your own pet-sitting business and don't know where to begin or you're practically a pro already, I hope this book can give you some insight and resources as to how to run a successful pet-sitting business.

Pet-sitting requires a special brand of patience, compassion, and dedication. It is very different (and I'd like to argue much more fun) than regular old baby-sitting. Not being able to flat-out ask or be told when a dog needs to be walked or fed, when a cat needs some extra loving, or heck, even if a turtle needs to be told how rockin' his shell is looking that day—affirms that pet-sitters need to be emotionally aware and detail-oriented.

Pets are often treated as equal family members—we celebrate their birthdays, cater to their quirks, and miss them when we travel. Families that own pets will often go out of their way to accommodate their loved ones and will place a great deal of trust in those that they choose to watch their pets during their absence.

"As the leading therapy animal organization providing the best therapy animal teams, we certainly recognize the power of the human-animal bond on human health and well-being. We applaud all opportunities for animals to impact human health while advocating for the animal's welfare."
— Pet Partners

Regardless of whether you are planning to specialize in a specific type of animal care and don't classify yourself as a "cat person" or a "dog person" per se, it is very likely that you will encounter a variety of pet personalities as well as the personalities among their owners. This book will go into detail as to how to deal with clients in a professional manner. Even if you're not old enough to legally drive a car yet, that doesn't mean that your services and quality of care can't rival even the most aged industry professionals. You're probably much younger and way more energetic than some of those old dogs out there in the business anyway, so go ahead; give them a run for their money.

This book will also provide you with a few sample documents to help you get started such as client agreements, a sample flier, advertising and social media techniques, and tips for expanding your business. You will also hear advice from some who have had notable experiences pet-sitting.

Starting a unique business such as pet-sitting at a younger age will also help you to strengthen your ability to handle numerous responsibilities, stay organized, provide care for various pets that may have special requirements, learn how to deal with adults maturely, and above all, have fun!

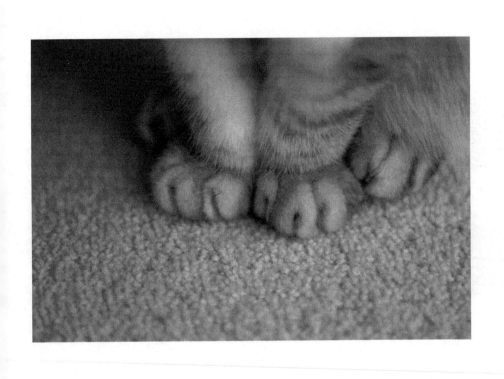

CHAPTER 1

Basics of Pet-Sitting

With any fresh new idea or daydream, it's always important to be realistic. Being realistic can even be enjoyable because planning ahead can be the difference between whether these ideas and dreams take off or come to a screeching halt.

Starting a pet-sitting business before going over some of the basic requirements of the job is like taking a 152-pound Doberman on a walk wearing roller-blades—you encounter one squirrel, and it's all over.

Do You Have What It Takes?

So you want to be a pet-sitter—fantastic! It's brave of you to want to dive into a field where cleaning up after another living thing and being slobbered and shed on are large components of the job. All of these things can be highly rewarding and well worth it, too; I can assure you.

Pet-sitting is an important profession because it allows owners to travel freely while leaving their pets in capable, caring hands. It is much easier on the pets, too, if they can remain among familiar surroundings even when their family may be away for longer periods of time. This way, a family's pet or pets can feel like the priority if they are tended to each day in their own home, rather than being lost in the shuffle of a large kennel or "pet resort."

That being said, there are also other responsibilities that may come with pet-sitting that don't involve remembering important medication or that Fluffy only likes being petted on her right back leg. This may include taking care of a family's mail, houseplants, or just watching over their home in general.

 Dalmatians are born pure white and develop black spots as they get older.[1]

To be a successful pet-sitter, you really have to love and appreciate animals. It is important that you are not only able to devote a considerable amount of time to their care, but also enjoy doing so. Some pets you encounter may be incredibly easy to manage and may always be in a great mood to see you.

---

1. www.petfinder.com

However, it is very likely that you may encounter some frustrating situations as well.

Ask yourself:

- Does getting covered in cat hair or dog slobber bother you?

- Do you mind if you get covered in muddy footprints?

- Do you enjoy spending time outside or going for long walks? How about a game of fetch?

- Are you able to tell when an animal needs attention or help?

- Do you usually get along well with animals?

- Are you willing to clean up after animals again and again?

Pet-sitting focuses on animal care, but you have to be able to relate to humans too. Owners' happiness is just as important as pet happiness — especially if you want to get paid. It is vital to the success of your business that you are not only a pet-pleaser but also a people-pleaser.

In all service professions, people are very much at the forefront. Whether it is dealing with difficult clients or finding new ones, your limits may be tested. It is important to remain open, accommodating, and patient throughout your career as a pet-sitter. Since you are going into peoples' homes and interacting pretty intimately in their lives, there are also important boundaries to consider. Make sure that what your client is asking of you is something a pet-sitter would do. Bringing in garbage cans or the mail every now and then is fine, but use discretion. If you're not careful, you could quickly become their personal assistant or housekeeper without any extra moolah!

Ask yourself:

- Are you comfortable approaching new clients and having interviews with them to see if you would be a good fit?

- Can you build relationships with clients and remain mindful of their needs?

- Are you willing to remain firm in your pricing agreements and details outlined on your agreement?

- Would you be able to discontinue serving a client if problems arose?

It is incredibly important that you come across as honest, confident, and knowledgeable. This is the only way that you will earn clients' trust because

FUN FACT   It's a myth that dogs only can see in black and white. It's believed that dogs primarily see in blue, greenish-yellow, yellow, and various shades of gray.[2]

Remember when I said that your young age actually puts you at an advantage? Here's another reason why: clients may be more inclined to choose you over "Granny Jean's Pet-Sitting Service" because they are confident that you can keep up with their rambunctious puppy or cluster of kittens. It is important for you to be in good health in order to take proper care of your clients' animals.

If any of the requirements of a proper pet-sitter sound daunting to you, perhaps it would make sense for you to gain some more animal-handling experience before you officially pull the trigger on starting a business. Consider volunteering at a local animal shelter or working at a pet-grooming salon. This will help you become more aware of your strengths and weaknesses when dealing with animals (and people!).

Common Job Duties

If you caught the subtle irony of the term "duties," you probably have a good idea of what a lot of pet-sitting entails—cleaning up after animals in every capacity. However, pet-sitters are more than just human litter-scoops. You may find yourself taking on a variety of roles in just one hour on the job. It is possible that in this seemingly short amount of time, you may schedule an interview with a new client, take one of your existing client's dogs out for a quick walk, deposit a check and monitor your account, and run to the local animal clinic for a prescription.

2. www.about.com

This all may seem like too much, but it is all quite possible. The manageability of your workload will also be up to your ability to schedule. You should be mindful of your personal limits and not overload yourself—this is where quality over quantity comes into play. If your schedule mainly allows you to work on weekends or after classes, then planning is essential.

If you know you are going to have a long day of work, consider preparing the night before. You should pack your vehicle with a service kit (which will be discussed in detail later), clients' keys, a snack or two if necessary (food is fuel, so really it's always necessary), a change of clothes or shoes, and anything else your heart desires. If you are walking or biking to your clients' homes, make sure you have a comfortable backpack that can hold everything you may need. It also may be a good idea to bring a folder of client information with you for each visit. That way, you can quickly refer to notes you should have jotted down at your client interview. You can also organize your notes on your phone, if you want to save the trees or whatever—but make sure your phone is charged in case of emergencies!

It is also important that you use your time efficiently. Map out your route for which client you will visit first, second, and so forth. That way, you can provide your services in a timely manner without exhausting yourself in the process. Time is money, as the old folks say (and they're right). Each pet visit may take anywhere from 30 minutes to an hour, and even more if your client has multiple pets or requests that you stay and keep their lonely pup or cat company.

A typical visit will include putting out fresh food, water, exercising or playing with the pet or pets, making sure they are healthy, and, of course, cleaning up after them. It is also a good idea to take notes during each visit or text their owner with an update if appropriate. It is also likely that you may have to visit the same pet more than once per day. You should check

over your schedule frequently to make sure you do not forget any visits, as this could be disastrous.

Meeting with potential clients will also be an important part of your daily duties. In these interviews, you will not only express to the client why you are qualified and should be hired, but you will also be gathering important information about them, their home, and their pets. It is typical during these interviews that the client will show you where all of their pet supplies are kept as well as a general meet-and-greet with their pet to become ac-quainted. When pet-owners are absent, you as a pet-sitter become the most important person in their pets' lives. If you feel that you will not be able to meet a client's needs, by all means, be honest. It's better for you to not sign an agreement with someone at all if you suspect that you will struggle with their pet later on.

FUN FACT   The proper name for a group of cats is a clowder. A group of kittens is called a kindle.[3]

As a pet-sitter, you will also have to advertise your business. This may include running a Facebook page or other social media sites, passing out fliers, or making phone calls. You will also be in charge of all of the money you earn or must spend on supplies. It is likely that every client will have enough supplies for you to use; however, it may be wise to invest in a few leashes or toys of your own. Consider keeping track of any money or mileage you rack up traveling to clients' homes. If you find that you are spending a lot, perhaps consider limiting the locations you serve, or increase your rates.

Types of pet-sitters and possible services

Below is a brief description of different types of pet-sitting roles you may fulfill or services you may provide. How you operate as a pet-sitter is ultimately up to you; however, the service you provide will most likely differ with each client.

1. Drop-in Service: A sitter goes to the pet-owner's home for one, two, or three visits per day. Average visits last 30 minutes for cat sits or 45 minutes for dog sits. This is the most common type.

---

3. www.more.com

2. Daily Dog Walking: A sitter provides walking services for pet-owners who work long hours that keep dogs cooped up. An average walk is 20 minutes, usually in the middle of the day. New puppies typically benefit from midday walk as well, since they may not be as accustomed to waiting all day to do their business or suppress their energy.

3. Picking Up Pet Supplies/Errands: It is reasonable for a client to ask a sitter to pick up food, litter, and medications. This service is less common, but if you are asked to do it, make sure you charge some sort of fee for mileage/gas or convenience.

4. Transportation to Vet or Groomers: A sitter drives a client's pet to an appointment. This is less common due to it being a hassle in most cases. This may not apply to you if you do not have access to a vehicle.

5. Grooming: A sitter bathes a dog with shampoo and towels provided by the owner. If the dog needs special grooming, the owner has already set this up. However, during your time taking care of the animal, they may need extra grooming. This is when it is important for you to keep dogs from playing in mud or dirt, or making sure you dry them off well if it raining outside—unless you want to create more work for yourself!

6. In-home Boarding: The pet stays in the sitter's home (that's your home, homie—or your parent's home, I guess). Be mindful of what pets you bring into your own home; this may be more of a hassle than it's worth. Some pets may be especially destructive if they're unfamiliar with you or this new environment. If you won't be able to spend considerable time with the pet or pets yourself, this effort may be counterintuitive. If you are that much of an expert (and your parents are that lenient), and you're keeping several pets at a time, you may even have to gain clearance from your neighborhood or community for a special kennel license.

7. Overnight Service: This one is pretty self-explanatory too. A sitter stays in the home from the evening hours until the next morning for about a 12-hour period, such as 7 p.m. to 7 a.m.

8. House Sitting: A sitter stays in the home the entire time during an owner's absence, 24 hours a day. This is less commonly offered, because the sitter cannot take on any other jobs, and it's incredibly time consuming.

Gaining Experience

The absolute best way to gain proper experience to become a pet-sitter is to be a pet-owner. If you don't enjoy or can't handle taking care of your own pet, then why on earth would you want to take care of anyone else's? But clearly, if you are still reading this, that's not the case. You, my friend, want to perpetually surround yourself with puppies, of course. Who wouldn't?

Being a pet-owner will automatically lead to more comfortable encounters among you, potential clients, and their pets. There is an unspoken presence and way about pet-lovers that dogs and cats read and pick up on and will generally respond incredibly well to. Their owners will pick up on it, too.

 Bark Break!
Don't let your ears hang low

There will be plenty of people who will tell you no in your life-time, who will doubt you, question you, and just flat-out make you bummed to be a human. There will be challenging pets, too, which may have odd or annoying quirks. This doesn't make them any less worthy of your time and attention. If any-thing, this means that they are more in need of your love and affection, as they may be acting out because their owner—their entire life, essentially—is missing and their sense of normalcy is drastically shaken.

Don't let any of it get you down, at least not for too long. It's pretty likely that if anyone (like one of your peers, for example) excessively dishes out unwanted beef to you for being a pet-sitter that they're just jealous. Any obstacle or difficult person placed in your life should be seen as an opportunity to grow, learn, or exert your awesomeness—'cause you've got a lot of it.

There are also many opportunities around your town that can provide you with additional experience and increase your comfort around pets. Besides volunteering at a pet groomer or shelter as I mentioned before, you can also visit a clinic and ask to help out there. In order to gain insight regarding proper nutrition, you can ask to shadow a pet specialty store employee. If you're lucky enough to have a pet show or training facility nearby, volunteer there.

Make sure that you also understand some basic training practices used for dogs and that you're mindful of the importance of body language. Watching *The Dog Whisperer* can help quite a bit, but attending an obedience school with your own pet will teach you invaluable skills. Imagine how well clients would respond if they came back from vacation to find that you have taught their spacey, hyperactive pup to properly heel or to sit!

FUN FACT Like most mammals, cats lose their ability to digest dairy after infancy—making them lactose intolerant.[4]

---

4. www.more.com

There is also a valuable organization called Pet Sitters International (PSI). PSI offers pet-sitters an accreditation program to sharpen their professional skills. An in-depth educational program teaches pet-sitters all they need to know about pet care, health and nutrition, business management, office procedures, and additional services. The top pet-sitting professionals in the industry have worked together to develop this coursework.

While you can learn this knowledge in other places, such as by reading this book, PSI offers accreditation for students completing this coursework. Your clients will know that by hiring an accredited sitter, they are assured of hiring a professional with in-depth knowledge of modern pet practices and skilled in caring for pets. To become accredited, the pet-sitter has to learn and exhibit a working knowledge of taking care of many types of animals and running an efficient business.

An accurate assessment of your abilities and strengths before you begin this new endeavor will help you to decide what's best for you. As you're finishing this first chapter, jot down some of your feelings (ew, right?). But seriously, write down what areas of the sitting biz you feel confident in already as well as some questions you hope to answer. Make a list of your personal strengths and weaknesses. How can you improve upon them before, during, and after your new era of dominating the pet-sitting world? As you continue to develop a clearer understanding of what is expected of you, it will become a lot easier to complete the next step: setting up your business plan and becoming a *boss* boss.

CHAPTER 2

Becoming the World's Best Boss

Well, you're thinking this is a pretty dumb concept, right? Of course you're going to love your boss — it is you, after all. However, you're wrong. Even in self-employed industries such as pet-sitting it's a little too common to want to give a swift kick in the pants to the person in charge — which is quite a sight to see.

As your own boss, you can either be your own hero or your own worst enemy. This has a lot to do with how much effort you're willing to put into the pre-planning and planning processes, day-to-day operations, self-evaluations, organization, and more. The more seriously you take yourself, the more seriously your clients will take you. If you really want to be successful as a pet-sitter, crack those knuckles and get ready to work. As I have discussed before, being a pet-sitter is *all* about the pets, but it also isn't. As a pet-sitter, you will have to be all things — a financial planner, a customer service rep, an assistant, a boss, a chef, a doctor, a historian, and most of all, a good companion.

Business Plan

Here we are, friend, about to get right down to it. I've already proverbially smacked you on the hand about the importance of planning your business model quite a bit — get excited for the details.

Naming and brand development

Names are important. That's why everyone has one, and we're not all just referred to by our social security number, which would make for a pretty crazy world. Think long and hard about what you want the name of your business to be—it'll be around for the long haul, or at least, as long as you're pet-sitting. If you struggle with creativity, simply call it "Reganne Yorkie's Pet-Sitting Service" (if your name is Reganne Yorkie, of course.) You get the idea. Using your own name for your business will automatically make it unique to you, which makes it easy for clients to remember your name and refer their friends to you.

The most successful mountain rescue dog ever was a St. Bernard named Barry, who saved more than 40 lives.[5]

If you do choose to use your complete name in the business, you won't need to register your name with your local city hall or town clerk's office. But if you have chosen a title that only includes part of your name, like "Reganne's Pet-Sitting Service," you will need to register the fact that you are doing business under another name (labeled "dba"). While this does not protect or trademark your name, it does allow the public to know who owns your business. Fees for this registration vary from state to state, but your city hall will have the information you need to register.

It should be noted that with any mentioned legal "stuff" in this book, it may or may not apply to you. If you plan on having a small-scale, low-client operation, then it is unlikely you will have to formally register your business or really involve anyone but yourself (or maybe your chauffeurs).

---

5. www.mspca.org

 **Bark Break!**
Bossing it up

Maybe you've never had a boss in your life besides one of your family members. But based off of this, TV, movies, and books you probably have a pretty good idea of what qualities make up a great or a not-so-great boss. What qualities fit into either category? How can you apply them to yourself? After all, you'll most likely just be in charge of yourself — will you be easy to manage?

If you have had a boss before, what did you learn from them? What do you wish you could forget about them? Maybe they were always super positive. Maybe they brought in donuts on the first day of every month. Or, maybe they had really bad personal hygiene. Maybe they made weird jokes or gave you a derogative or annoying nickname, like Spunky.

Coming into your own as a boss and business owner is an exciting opportunity to exhibit leadership strategies you've admired about your role models in the past. Maybe it is a monthly donut that keeps you going or maybe you like to post motivational notes and images all over your room.

If you do decide to go the creative route, make sure that the name you are considering is not already in use or does not sound similar to another business name. The last thing you would want is to be compared to a sub-par pet-sitter of a similar name or with bad street cred. If another corporation already uses that name, you will not be able to use it either. The US Patent and Trademark Office (PTO) or a business attorney can inform you on whether another business has already registered your business name; if this is not the case, go ahead and obtain the PTO forms and trademark your business name. If you don't, and another company registers it you will be legally required to change your name. This action will compel you to print up new stationery, business cards, and brochures.

That being said, your brand is also equally as important as the name of your business. What exactly is a "brand," though? We're not just talking things like Nike or Kellogg's Raisin Bran—even though these are both icons in their own way. Your "brand" is essentially everything associated with your business, not just your name. It encompasses everything about it—what area you service, what kind of reputation you have, how you represent your business and your persona, how expensive your services are, logos, advertising and social media habits, etc. Some of your brand will develop right when you start your business; however, most of it will develop as time goes on and you gain more experience.

Outlining your plan

Think of creating this outline like getting your wisdom teeth out—it may suck initially, but you'll be much happier and pain-free in the long run. Since you want to become a pet-sitter, you're obviously more of a doer. Drafting a plan for anything may sound horrendous, but, if done right, it can actually be fun. There is an example business plan filled out for you in the back of this book.

1. Business summary

   a. Objectives

   b. Mission statements

   c. Keys to success

2. Management summary

   a. Goals as your own boss

   b. Terms for your assistants (if applicable)

3. Products and services

   a. Product and service descriptions

   b. Technology you will use

   c. Future products and services

4. Check out the competition

5. Service area

   a. Area needs

   b. Future growth

6. Strategy for services

   a. Competitive edge

   b. Marketing/Promotional strategy

      i. Social Media

7. Establishing price

   a. Initial costs

   b. Operational costs

   c. What you will charge

Business summary

Have I scared you away? Man (or woman) up and get back here. These terms may sound a bit intimidating or irrelevant, but they aren't. Just take it one thing at a time, and you'll be done before you know it. First, write down a summary of what your business is and what it will offer. This summary will also be used as a 30-second personal commercial or "elevator pitch," so be creative and descriptive.

Not everyone has heard of pet-sitting as a business, and you have the opportunity to introduce people to the industry while you possibly attract a client. Write down some objectives and mission statements. These are pretty much one in the same, but they differ slightly in that objectives make up your mission statement and are more short-term, whereas your mission statement is a long-term goal for where you want your business to go. It's also a good idea to jot down a few keys to success, whatever this may mean for you. It could be that you should remind yourself to maintain a positive attitude or that you will attempt to sign a new client every two months.

 It's estimated that 70–80 million dogs and 74–96 million cats are owned in the United States. [6]

Management summary

Next, you should detail a brief management summary. What kind of boss do you want to be? Are you going to enlist help from family members or friends? These are important things to consider. What areas do you believe you can improve upon in terms of being self-sufficient and successful? This is a good place to outline some personal and professional goals. It's important to jot a few down and then revisit them later on to measure your progress. Self-evaluation and goal setting are valuable tools that you will use the rest of your life. You know your own strengths and weaknesses and you are, whether this makes sense or not, the only person standing in the way of your own success.

---

6. www.aspca.org

Products and services

You should then consider your products and services. The notion of products may not be as applicable to you—unless you plan on making your own brand of homemade cat treats. What services are you planning to offer? Are you going to start off with a few and then add more later on? It would be helpful to refer back to the types of pet-sitting in Chapter 1 for ideas. Next, consider technology. What type of devices or apps are you going to use? It may be beneficial to use your phone to record quick notes about particular clients as well as all of their contact information. It is also wise to keep hard copies as well as digital copies on your computer. Dropbox is a great tool to be able to access important files from anywhere, and it's also available in a convenient, free app for mobile devices. Technology will also come into play a lot in the promotional section. Next, think of the future—even though it is difficult. Do you see yourself being a pet-sitter for years and growing your client base to serve your entire zip code?

Check out the competition

Next, don't be daunted or discouraged by checking out the competition. Instead, look at it as a way to know how to better arm yourself against other pet-sitters who may try to steal your clients. How do they have an edge over you? How can you have an edge over them? Do some research. You may want to consider listing yourself on Rover, an app that connects pet-owners to pet-sitters based on their location and preferences. Download Rover for yourself; it's free. See who's working in your area.

Service area

For the service area section, the answer is pretty self-explanatory and all up to you. How large a region do you want to be available in? Do you just want to serve your neighborhood or would you be OK going across town every once in a while? Again, think of the future. Do you plan to expand? It would be wise to include this when you advertise your company on social media as well. If someone is looking for a pet-sitter in Florida and your business comes up, but the interested client lives in Miami and you live in Tampa, this wouldn't work. It's important to provide some sort of spatial context. For example, "Matthew's Pet-Sitting: Servicing North Tampa Neighborhoods." It's important to consider, as I have mentioned before, how much travel time you will be required to do in order to visit clients. Don't stretch yourself too thin or over too large an area; it will be incredibly difficult to provide good care if you spend your entire day juggling different clients and being stuck in traffic.

Strategy for services

Consider your strategy for services, this ties back into your competition. Think of ways you can set yourself apart and exemplify a business that's a cut above your competition. What are some unique perks you can offer your clients and their pets? Is it making homemade cat treats? Perhaps the next topic on your outline is one of the most important—your marketing strategy. How are you planning on getting the word out about your business? You should always start small and then work your way up. Begin by asking around among family and friends and among friends of friends and friends of family—you get the idea. You are more likely to have success with signing clients initially if someone you know can throw in a quick reference and gush about how awesome you are with pets (and in general).

Marketing and social media

Facebook, Twitter, Instagram, and even Snapchat are all great marketing tools right at your fingertips that you already know how to use (I'm assuming). Facebook, Twitter, and Instagram can easily be used to coordinate posts from your business about specials you are offering (maybe a complimentary bath) or fun updates about the pets you are taking care of. Be mindful of both client and pet privacy, however, and do not post anything that would reveal too much about your client being out of town or where they live.

FUN FACT Dogs' nose prints are as unique as human fingerprints and can be used to identify them.[7]

Even though privacy settings on all of these social media sites can be easily manipulated to make you "secure," you never know what information can seep through these supposed digital brick walls. Having a Facebook page just for your business can also be helpful in terms of contacting clients and having

---

7. www.boredpanda.com

them contact you. Facebook, Twitter, and Instagram can also all be used to research potential clients by following friends, family, and mutual friends.

Budgeting

Now let's talk about money, honey. Even though you're getting into the pet-sitting business because you enjoy taking care of animals — not necessarily to stretch out your wallet or add commas on commas to your bank account — it still needs to be worth your while and effort. And that old adage rings true that "time is money." We discussed earlier how long you might spend taking care of a client's pet for a variety of different services.

Initial and operational expenses

I hate to break it to you, but sometimes you have to spend money to make money (actually, pretty much all the time). It is important to consider some initial costs and operational costs that will go into starting your pet-sitting business. You want to start off on the right foot, and professionally so. Think about things like supplies and transportation. Your clients will probably have everything to keep their pets healthy and happy already, but that may not always be the case. You may have to bring your own leash, toys, or cleaning supplies as a back up. There are also other supplies that aren't necessarily pet-related that you may need. This includes office supplies and organizational tools such as binders, folders, and notebooks (if you're more old school) to keep your business running smoothly. You may also want to spend a bit on business cards or fliers to pass out around your neighborhood or town events, such as festivals or sporting events. Have your friends and family bring a flier or two to work as well.

Transportation costs

Transportation is probably the single most important tool you have. Will you be walking, biking, blading, driving, or taking the bus to your clients? Do you have a reliable back up if any of these options fail? If you use a car often, you will obviously have to spend more on gas and check-ups. If you use a bike often, you may need to pay for repairs. Keep this in mind. Whatever kind of transportation you have will also affect what services you can provide and what clients you gain. A client may want a pet-sitter that has his or her own car and is able to take their pet out to the park, run an errand, or, in case of emergency, take their pet to the vet. Conversely, some clients may prefer if you are a close neighbor and can simply walk over to their home. These initial, operational, and transportation costs should factor into your price, which we'll get into next.

Adding up your worth

Pet-sitting experts agree that the basic pet-sitting appointment takes about 30 minutes to an hour, including driving or transportation time. During that basic visit, a sitter will usually exercise or walk the pets, check their health, feed them, give them water, bring in any mail or newspapers, and water plants. As a sitter, you will check the house for obvious signs of entry or danger, change the position of drapes or blinds, or perhaps switch on different lights so that the house appears occupied. However, some sitters offer further services, such as grooming, brushing, or bathing. Some sitters offer to stay overnight with the animals. Another sitter might water or mow lawns or take care of the garden while the owners are gone. Adding on a trip to the vet or an obedience lesson will allow you to add on extra charges to the bill.

Also, once you set a basic rate for an appointment, it's necessary to consider how you will handle additional animals. Many clients you meet are likely to have more than one pet in the house, and your fee schedule should take this into account. Clients may try to get you to care for other pets for free.

Some pets, such as cats, may take just a little of your time to care for, and they may argue that it only takes a few minutes to check on a hamster and give it some food and water. However, this is time that you could spend on another appointment whose client is paying you full price. Do not sell your time cheap; you're worth more than that! You may want to add a small charge ($2-$5 per visit or per day) for easy-care animals like cats that will entertain and exercise themselves, or a flat fee for each additional pet.

According to my calculations . . .

Finally, consider whether you will charge more for holiday visits. Some sitters do charge more; they consider the time they are taking away from their own families and consider it a common business practice to charge more for premium times. Other sitters consider that their clients are most likely to use sitting services during holidays, and thus a base rate is reasonable. How much profit will you expect to make? First, you should consider the value of your time. If you could be working as a cashier for $9 an hour, your profit opportunity is $9 an hour. Thus, for an hour-long pet-sitting visit, you could reasonably charge about $12, which includes your $3 cost of transportation or convenience fee and your $9 opportunity.

 **FUN FACT** When playing with female puppies, male puppies will often let them win, even if they're at a physical advantage.[8]

You also need to determine what people are willing to pay. First, you can check with other pet-sitters in your area or do some research with pet-sitting organizations. Consider whether your area has an average cost of living or is higher/lower than the average: urban areas tend to be higher and rural areas tend to be lower. This is important information to help adjust your rates against a national average (because it's all about the big picture).

Once you have determined a base rate, you can then add to it for special services. Extra items, such as grooming or longer walks, might be charged according to your hourly rate or rate per visit. For example, if you charge $12 a visit for a half-hour appointment, but also walk the dog an additional 15 minutes, you can charge an extra $6 for the 15-minute walk. In determining the basic rate, you plan a 30-minute visit and 30 minutes of travel time. If it takes longer to get to and from your client's house than 15 minutes, you may want to charge extra for the visit. An easy way to do this is to refer back to your service area you defined. Your basic zone might be 10 miles or less from your home. A client who is 10 to 20 miles from home might be an expanded service zone for which you charge extra—say, mileage reimbursement (number of miles x current government rate of $0.54 a mile) or an additional fee of $10 per visit. Finally, you will need to get a key

8. www.boredpanda.com

from the client before the first visit, so you will want to consider whether you will absorb the cost of the travel or whether you will charge a fee for retrieval and drop-off of keys.

There are two other considerations on setting fees: whether the fees are too high or low, and whether you have specific income needs that must be met. If you have a specific income need that is not met by your planned rate structure, you will need to determine whether you will work longer hours, cut costs, or charge more to meet your goals. If you set your fees too low, you may not necessarily attract more customers, and your profit may be too small to be sustainable. If you set fees too high, your clients may not see enough value to want to hire you—or may not want to contact you a second time.

Bark Break!
The importance of treating yo'self

"Treating yo'self" hasn't become a revered proverb of the 21st century for nothing. Buying yourself something large or small every once in a while is a great way to stay motivated — whether it's a pair of sneakers you've been coveting for a year or a few scoops of your favorite ice cream you've been coveting for a few hours — after some hard work, go for it.

You may choose to schedule these small indulgences after a passage of time or after earning a certain amount of money. Or, in all honesty, if you find yourself down in the dumps but doing well in the pet-sitting business, treat yo'self for the morale boost alone. There is great power in positive reinforcement. Whatever you need to do to prove to yourself or to others that your efforts aren't for nothing — do it.

Of course, you can always re-evaluate rates once you are established or when you have new credentials or services. When you change rates, though, you will have to re-publish any materials that showed your original rates. You may also have difficulty with current clients who are satisfied and comfortable with current charges, but who may be unwilling to pay for an increase.

Once you have set your rates, it is a good business practice to stick to them as much as possible. Why? Client agreements. Your clients expect honesty and consistency. We'll talk about those next.

Also, you may run into trouble if you give a friend a discounted rate, and then he or she quotes that rate to people he or she has referred to you. You should treat all of your clients fairly. At other times, though, you may sit for a client that requires little to no traveling (such as a neighbor across the street), and you may feel uncomfortable including a travel cost in his or her rate.

Some visits may take substantially more effort than you originally estimated, and you may need to re-negotiate. Rule with an iron (but courteous) fist. To give yourself some wiggle room, you might consider quoting a new client a range of prices, rather than a set rate.

When you have a specific rate structure defined, you must think about the policies that you will have in place to handle payment. Some sitters require full payment in advance, while others ask for a deposit and then receive the balance after the work is completed. You will also want to consider whether you will charge the client for a missed interview or a cancellation. While that may sound a little harsh, during busy times you may be completely booked and need to turn away requests for appointments. If someone cancels his or her appointments at the last minute, you are losing money unless you can fill those hours. This is a standard business practice among many professionals, like doctors and lawyers who charge by the appointment, and you are every bit the professional that they are.

Payment policies

Since you're running this ship, it's entirely up to you how and when you expect your clients to pay you. It may be wise to adopt a blanket policy for everyone right away and lay it out for your clients. That way, no one will feel comfortable about paying you a month later or at their leisure—even if you are that calm and cool about it.

In the past, having a few pet-sitting jobs here and there may have rendered cash payments useful and convenient. However, you're in the big leagues now. It's time to talk to mom or dad or whoever helps you survive on a daily basis about opening a checking account or creating a joint checking account. The latter are often set up for young adults who are still dependent by definition but independent by nature — or who are just ready for a bit of financial responsibility.

If you do accept payment by cash, it is really important to record each transaction carefully. Cash is harder to trace than any other form of payment. Be sure that you have a receipt book, and give one copy to your client while keeping one for yourself. If you have a number of clients who like to pay by cash, you will need to make more frequent stops at the bank to deposit your earnings, since carrying large amounts of cash is not a good idea.

Doing so will make it incredibly easy for you to manage your own money and deposit payments from clients. Many major banks have mobile apps that allow you to deposit checks from images alone, and the funds show up shortly in your account — available for withdrawal or linked to a debit card. These mobile apps also allow you to track your spending with ease and keep you deep into the green and out of the red.

You may also consider PayPal[9], an online payment service that offers quite a bit in flexibility and convenience. The company is designed to transfer money from buyer to seller online through accounts that each party sets up. The money is removed directly from the buyer's checking, savings, or credit card account and deposited to any of those accounts that the seller owns. Accounts are secure and easy to set up. With a few mouse clicks, clients can send payments directly to your bank account!

---

9. www.paypal.com

If you're feeling particularly modern and secure in your savvy-ness, you may also consider an app called FreshBooks[10], which is a cloud-based accounting software. You don't have to jump into a program like this right away. This can be used as you sign more clients since it allows you to more easily manage an excess of payments. FreshBooks also allows you to invoice clients, have clients pay you online with cards, and track your expenses and growth over time.

Regardless of whether you choose a program like this, taking a quick survey of how it works can help you think like an accountant and more appropriately manage all of your finances. You should review all payments and withdrawals on a monthly if not weekly basis. You should also always keep track of how much you are expected to earn versus how much you actually earn, just to make sure no wily customers are shorting you.

_____

10. www.freshbooks.com

Some Quick Business Do's And Don'ts

Do:

1. Price your services appropriately. Complete a survey of the pet-sitting businesses already around you to price your service. You can find sitters in your area by researching social media or by using Rover or a similar app. Also, try a search of pet sitters through the Pet Sitters International website[11] or the National Association of Professional Pet Sitters website.[12] Call pet stores, veterinary hospitals, and groomers near your home, and ask if they recommend any local pet-sitting businesses. Go to local pet stores, vets, and groomers to see if they have any cards on display. When you contact local sitters, say, "I am a new pet-sitting business owner, and I want to price my services appropriately. Would you mind telling me what you charge? Also, I would like to network with someone in my area to refer to when I am taking time off or am overbooked. Are you on Facebook or other social media, and can you send me some more information?"

2. Network with other sitters. Many sitters have reported that a significant number of all their clients come from referrals from other pet-sitting companies they have networked with or met through professional associations. You can all be friends and still be competitive.

3. Limit your area of coverage. Start with no more than a 10-mile radius from your home, and decrease that area as you have sufficient clients within a smaller radius. Remember, your profit is dependent on how far you drive and time you spend traveling.

---

11. **www.petsit.com**
12. **www.petsitters.org**

FUN FACT

A cat cannot break a sweat because they don't have sweat glands.[13]

4. Determine your maximum number of appointments. If you are a full-time sitter, with all your appointments within a 10-mile radius of your home, the most appointments you could possibly book in one day is 14 individual sits. However, if you did that many for long, you would burn out. A full-time sitter has 10 visits a day during the busy season and four visits a day during the slow season.

5. Avoid burnout. If you're struggling to balance school, extracurricular activities, or even another job, ask for help or take on fewer clients. Reach out to some of those pet-sitting buds you made and perhaps ask for a cut of their profits for the tip. You may have a personal emergency or need to take some time off; having a go-to colleague to cover for you is invaluable.

6. Be patient with your business growth. If you're smart about your business plan and conscientious about your spending, you will reap the benefits in no time.

Don't:

1. Price other sitters out of the market. You may think that charging less than the other sitters will drive customers to you, but this can be a big mistake. Pet owners may wonder why you are the cheapest service in town. You might also end up with clients other sitters don't want to take. Finally, this is not a high-paying job to begin with, and if you price your services below market rate, you are setting a low value on your time and skills. Own it!

---

13. www.animalleague.org

2. Print too many forms or fliers or buy too many supplies before you start making money. Printers will always be around, and your supplies aren't going to go extinct. Additionally, you may want to make corrections and additions to your information after you've been in business a while, and it may be harder to justify printing up new promotional materials when you have plenty. Not to mention, social media posts are free and can be edited (for free too). Another great case for social media is that it is illegal—yes, you heard it here—to put fliers in mailboxes without stamps, and it is inconsiderate to put fliers under car windshields in parking lots. Most people do not appreciate that and will probably throw them away! Instead, try to hand-deliver fliers to people around your town or neighborhood. That way, they can put a face with your business and maybe offer you their business right on the spot. Or, best-case/worst-case scenario, they deny your business, and that's one more flier you can give to someone who will appreciate it.

3. Have one lone copy of any given important document. Always keep back-up copies of important documents. Take photos of them on your phone if you're too lazy to upload them digitally—which you should do eventually anyway. Use Dropbox; it may save your life.

4. Overbook pet sits. There are unethical sitters who overbook appointments in such numbers that they could not possibly care for all the animals each day. Instead, they visited the pets every other day or every third day of the job. This is considered fraud, and sitters who engage in this practice will ruin their business, reputation, and face extreme consequences.

5. Refer problem animals or clients. If you have struggled with a non-paying client, a filthy home, or a dangerous animal, do not refer them to another sitter to get out of the job. This unethical behavior will ruin your reputation and could put another sitter in danger.

6. Criticize other sitters or clients. Today, there are many ways to communicate and network, including social media, associations, and industry

websites. Whatever you post in these places is public information that anyone can read; your words will reflect positively or negatively on your business. Always be professional and gracious, and handle conflicts person-to-person.

Client Agreements

If you want to be taken seriously, having a professional client agreement will say a lot about you. Your clients will appreciate having a physical copy of all of the terms of your agreement—how many visits you will pay their pet, what each visit will entail, how long your services will last, any additional costs or perks, and, most importantly, how much they should expect to owe you. The last thing you would want is to make your client unhappy or mislead them about what is reasonable for them to expect from you.

Having a solid agreement in place and tweaking as needed for every client you serve can save you from countless headaches and nights spent sobbing over a pint of ice cream. There is a sample agreement in the back of this book as well as below for your convenience. Client agreements will be covered again in Chapter 4. They should be filled out during client interviews to further strengthen communication and limit misunderstandings.

Sample Client Agreement

(Company Name) Pet Sitting Service Agreement

Contact Information _____

Note: If something does not apply to you or your home, please indicate by entering "N/A" in the space.

Name: _____

Email address: _____

Home Phone: _____

Business Phone: _____

Address: _____

Who else has access to your home? Please write name and phone numbers.

Your Landlord: _____

Maid/Cleaning Service: _____

Other: _____

Describe Your Pet(s)

If you have more than three pets, please attach additional information at bottom of sheet.

Pet's Name and species:

1) _____ 2) _____ 3) _____

Sex:

1) _____ 2) _____ 3) _____

Favorite toys/treats:

1) _____ 2) _____ 3) _____

Number of visits per day: _____

Sample Pet Information Form

Owner's name: _____

Home #: _____ Cell #: _____ Work #: _____

Address: _____

Designated Emergency Pet Guardian: _____

Home #: _____ Cell #: _____ Work #: _____

E-mail address: _____

Address: _____

Pet's name: _____

Dog   Cat   Other   (circle one)

Breed: _____ Sex: Male   Female   Age: _____

Spayed/Neutered: Yes   No   County Tag ID: _____

ID Microchip: Yes   No   If yes, Microchip #: _____

Weight: _____ Height: _____ Eye color: _____ Tail: _____

Hair color: _____ Hair length: _____

Veterinarian office: _____

Vet's name: _____ Phone #: _____

Date of last vaccinations: _____

Any medical conditions/allergies? _____

Any special medications? _____

General disposition:

Is your pet good around children?   Yes   No

Is your pet good around dogs?   Yes   No

Is your pet good around cats?   Yes   No

Specific identifying marks and/or features that would help to ID your pet:

_____

_____

List of people who could identify your pet:

1. Name _____ Phone _____

2. Name _____ Phone _____

General Pet Care Information

PLEASE NOTE: The utmost care will be given in watching both your pet(s) and your home. However, due to the extreme unpredictability of animals, we cannot accept responsibility for any mishaps of any extraordinary or unusual nature (i.e. biting, furniture damage, accidental death, etc.) or any complications in administering medications to the animal. Nor can we be liable for injury, disappearance, death or fines of pet(s) with access to the outdoors.

Vet Preference: _____

Phone: _____

Are pets secured in home or yard? : _____

Terms and Conditions

This is the agreement part; please fill in all the blanks and be sure to read carefully.

1. The parties herein agree as follows: The initial term of this agreement shall be from _____ through _____

In the event of early return home, client must notify Pet Sitter promptly to avoid being charged for unnecessary visits(s).

2. The baseline fee is (hare per visit) x (number of visits) for a total of _____ .

Other fees for additional services or circumstances may apply. Any additional visits made or services performed shall be paid for at the agreed rate. Pet Sitter is authorized to perform care and services as outlined on this document. Pet Sitter is also authorized by Client (name entered below) to seek emergency veterinary care with release from all liabilities related to transportation, treatment, and expense.

3. Should specified veterinarian be unavailable, Pet Sitter is authorized to approve medical and/or emergency treatment (excluding euthanasia) as

recommended by a veterinarian. Client agrees to reimburse Pet Sitter/Company for expenses incurred, plus any additional fee for attending to this need or any expenses incurred for any other home/food/supplies needed.

4. In the event of inclement weather or natural disaster, Pet Sitter is entrusted to use best judgment in caring for pet(s) and home. Pet Sitter/Company will be held harmless for consequences related to such decisions.

5. Pet Sitter agrees to provide the services stated in this agreement in a reliable, caring and trustworthy manner. Inconsideration of these services and as an express condition thereof, the client expressly waives and relinquishes any and all claims against said Pet Sitter/Company except those arising from negligence or willful misconduct on the part of the Sitter/Company.

6. Client understands this agreement also serves as an invoice and takes full responsibility for PROMPT payment of fees upon completion of agreed-upon services . A finance charge of ___percent per month will be added to unpaid balances after 30 days. A handling fee ($20) will be charged on all returned checks. One half deposit is required on lengthy assignments, and first time clients or clients with a history of late payment will be required to pay in advance before services are rendered. In the event it is necessary to initiate collection proceedings on the account, Client will be responsible for all attorney's fees and costs of collection.

7. In the event of personal emergency or illness of Pet Sitter, Client authorizes Pet Sitter to arrange for another qualified person to fulfill responsibilities as set forth in this agreement.

Client will be notified in such a case.

8. All pets are to be currently vaccinated. Should Pet Sitter be bitten or otherwise exposed to any disease or ailment received from Client's animal, which has not been properly and currently vaccinated, it will be the client's responsibility to pay all costs and damages incurred by the victim.

9. Pet Sitter/Company reserves the right to terminate this agreement at any time before or during its term. If Pet Sitter/Company, in its sole discretion, determines that Client's pet poses a danger to health or safety of Pet Sitter, if concerns

CHAPTER 3

Caring for Your Clients

Go ahead and crack those knuckles and get ready to work, friend—this will probably be the most important chapter we will cover. Without loyal clients or customers in any service industry profession, you simply won't have a business. Since you're just starting out, it's important to remember that you shouldn't be shooting for a huge quantity of clients—at least not right away. Your ambition should instead lie in providing premier quality care for a few valued pets and their owners. This way, you can get to know your clients and gain their trust as well as build strong bonds with their pets—probably so much so that they'll start to miss you when you're not around just like the rest of their family members! Starting small will easily allow you to get referred by your clients to their friends, neighbors, and family members as well. They will appreciate how much time and attention you are willing to give to them versus over-loading yourself and taking on 23 different dogs named Rufus or 81 cats name Fluffy (and be expected to differentiate between them all).

Meeting New Clients

Breathe. Just breathe. If you are really serious about being successful as a pet-sitter, you are obviously passionate about pet care and pet well-being. Let this passion shine through when you meet potential clients and interview them about their needs and their pet's needs. If you are positive and excited about the opportunity to take care of their pets, they will be excited to choose you as their sitter.

According to the American Kennel Club, the top breed of dog from 2013-2016 was Labrador Retriever.[14]

Conducting a client interview

Interviewing, at its core, is just a conversation with another human be-ing—there's nothing to stress about. The easiest way to quell nerves about an interview is to make sure that you prepare no later than the day before. If you use a client agreement as a guide like we discussed in Chapter 2, the interview will be a piece of cake. What exactly goes into preparing though? It's not as hard as it sounds. Here are few tips on preparing:

1. Make sure you have your paperwork in order (client agreement, extra paper for notes, a questionnaire, or whatever you choose).

2. Put your paperwork in a safe place, such as in a folder (and don't forget it or lose it!). You can also choose to use a laptop or tablet and fill out forms digitally. Some clients may ask for a copy of the agreement they sign, so keep this in mind.

3. Bring some sort of bag or accordion folder to keep clients' keys in if they choose to hand them over right away. Bring extra pens and perhaps a mini-stapler to seal the deal.

4. Dress professionally. You only have one chance to make a good first impression, and wearing ratty old gym clothes won't do the trick. Your client will appreciate the effort. You don't have to go full-tuxedo or ball gown, but at least wear jeans (not ripped) or pants and a nice shirt, or a

---

14. www.akc.org

dress or skirt (if that applies to you). When you are actually on the job your dress code is whatever you please, especially if you're dealing with messy pets.

5. Get a good night's sleep and take care of yourself. Eat some vegetables for goodness' sake (but I guess this advice goes for anything). If you're still wired right before your interview, listen to your favorite music on the drive or walk over to your client's home. Again, breathe.

You should want to find out some basic information about your client and each of their pets if they have more than one. Make sure to ask if there are any special instructions for any of their pets and jot these down. Keep these notes in a bound folder. It's a good idea to take handwritten notes with your client as you're filling out their agreement and then later type or scan these notes into your computer or save onto your phone for additional copies. This way, if all of your clients' contact information is stored in your phone, you know that you will always have access to it (because let's face it, your phone is always on you). Make sure to ask if there are any concerns your client has and do your best to assert that their pet would be in good hands under your care. Ask them if they have ever used a different pet-sitter before and if there is any way for you to exceed the level of service they have received in the past. Also, ask them if they have any questions for you. They may be unsure about signing something on your agreement or when you will expect payment. Below is a sample questionnaire for your client pro-file; make sure to fill out one per pet.

Pet Q&A

1. What is your pet's name? How old is he/she? _____

2. Is there anything this pet especially loves (playing fetch, back-scratches, etc.)?
   _____

3. Is there anything this pet dislikes (loud noises, bicycles, other dogs or cats,
   etc.)? _____

4. Does this pet need any special medical attention or medicine? _____
   _____

5. How often does this pet need to be taken outside or played with? How long do
   walks usually last? Is there a route this pet likes? _____
   _____

6. Is there any area of the house this pet isn't allowed in? Any furniture the pet
   isn't allowed on? _____

7. How many meals or treats should this pet get in a day? _____

8. Where are the supplies for this pet (food, leash, toys, litter box, etc.)?
   _____

9. Do you have any questions for me regarding our agreement or payment?
   _____
   _____

10. Is there anything else I should know to better care for your pet?
    _____
    _____

Some of the questions may not apply in all situations, but start thinking of questions you may have for a potential client before you sit down with them. If you are unsure of anything regarding a pet, you shouldn't be afraid to ask and even call for follow-up before your visits begin. Your client will appreciate your intention to be thorough.

Asking your clients how they heard about you (if it wasn't already clear) may also be a good idea. This way, if you are getting good exposure through some sort of outlet (like word-of-mouth, Twitter, Facebook, etc.) you should make sure to keep updated information on your business available.

If you haven't invested in business cards, make sure you give your potential client all your contact information. Let them know if you are unavailable during certain times of the day (if you have class or another job) and when they should expect a response from you. If they consider your services but do not sign with you right away, make sure to follow-up with them after your interview a few days later to express your interest in taking them on as a client.

A group of parrots is known as a pandemonium.[15]

Visiting Procedures

Not to scare you away, but pet-sitting is a pretty big responsibility. Owners are entrusting you with the keys to their home and the livelihood of creatures they consider family members—so much can go wrong, but even more can go right. In order to keep a handle on some basic, yet important tasks that may slip your mind, it's a good idea to keep a checklist with you

---

15. www.mnn.com

for each visit. Later on, we will get into detail about a variety of different pets, and the expectations of care for each of them. However, a broader checklist is provided for you below that you should use (either as a physical paper or on your phone) with every visit—no matter how many or what kinds animals you are caring for.

Visit Checklist

☐ I have all the proper keys and supplies (phone, pet profile or notes, extra leash, etc.).

☐ I know where my client's home is or I have a way of getting directions.

☐ I have checked to make sure my client's home looks safe to enter and there is nothing that appears suspicious.

☐ I have checked the interior of my client's home to make sure there is nothing that appears suspicious.

☐ I have taken care of all pets; walked them, fed them, replaced water for them, cleaned litter boxes, picked up their business in the yard, etc.

☐ I have disposed of any trash and cleaned up any messes.

☐ I have closed up food and medicine containers.

☐ I have made sure to put all pets back in the areas where they are allowed or back in their cages, if applicable.

☐ I have brought in mail and newspapers, watered plants, etc., if applicable.

☐ I have turned lights on or off

☐ When exiting, I made sure to lock up all doors and windows.

☐ I made sure I did not forget any of my personal belongings.

What's in a service kit?

Service kits will have different definitions for different people, but, really, it's just an easier way of saying a compilation of everything you'll need to do your job well and enjoy doing so. This can go beyond basic supplies that are a given for being a pet-sitter. Below are a few suggestions of what to pack for every visit or long day on the job.

- Jacket

- Umbrella

- Client keys (on a keychain you won't lose)

- Extra leash and a toy or two

- Some sort of snack or packed lunch (a protein bar, a piece of fruit, some crackers, nuts, etc.)

- Water or other beverages

- Cleaning wipes

- A few treats for either dogs or cats

- Client agreements or profile folder

- Cell phone and charger

- Hand sanitizer

- Wallet and car keys

- Sunglasses

- A book to pass the time

- Pen and notepad

- Extra business cards or fliers

- A first aid kit

- Flashlight

- Self-addressed and stamped envelopes to leave if your client must mail your payment

Basic Types of Care

Since you are the owner and operator of your business, you make the ultimate decision regarding what types of animals you feel comfortable taking care of. Here is breakdown of expectations for a variety of common household pets. The common factor among all pet care is that you should treat these pets even better than if they were your own, with love, attention, companionship, and patience.

 Dogs

- Every dog will require to be taken out several times per day. Only in very rare cases do dog owners have some sort of set-up indoors for their dog to do its business. Some people also have doggy doors that you may have to keep in mind. Whether a dog will require a short or long walk during these times will be determined by the dog's age or energy level.

- Most dogs will require playtime. Make sure to check with your client where their dog's toys are kept; however, it wouldn't hurt to bring a ball or fetch stick of your own.

- Make sure you bring an extra leash for backup. You never know if your client accidentally left their dog's leash in a weird spot—and you don't want to go snooping through their entire home to find it.

- Most dogs will require multiple meals and treats per day along with a few bowls of water. Make sure you know where all of their food is kept. If you plan to bring a different brand of treats with you, make sure to check with their owner beforehand. Some dogs have food allergies just like people.

- Many dogs, especially older dogs, require vitamin supplements such as glucosamine to help their joints. Make sure you're aware of these or any other medications your client's dog may need.

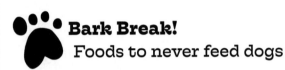

Bark Break!
Foods to never feed dogs

You may be thinking most dogs are pretty much invincible, right? Surely there's nothing that could harm them—especially any food, no matter how human or processed or just plain weird. However, here are a few common foods that you should keep out of paws reach, and never willingly give as a treat or handout. If a dog does come across any of these items in a very limited quantity, a rushed hospital visit is not necessary, but make sure to keep an eye out and keep the dog hydrated.

- Chocolate
- Onions and garlic
- Grapes and raisins
- Mushrooms (especially wild varieties)
- Alcohol
- Caffeine
- Dairy products
- Walnuts and macadamia nuts
- Artificial sweeteners
- Avocado

Also, be aware of azaleas and lilies while you're out walking, as these can be poisonous to dogs as well.[16]

Even though it may seem obvious to keep dogs away from snacking on non-food items, it's still important to be wary of household products or personal effects that owners may leave lying around. Here are a few things to watch out for.

• Kleenex, napkins, paper towels, etc.
• Socks, sandals, shoes, etc.
• Children's toys or stuffed animals
• Old newspapers

It's important to use your judgment in every situation as well. Even though owners may tell you their dogs are well-behaved, some dogs may become more stressed or frazzled than usual if their owners go away—the perfect recipe for trouble. Spending a few extra minutes checking your clients' homes can possibly save you a lot of hassle.

Cats

• Unlike dogs, most cats do not need to be taken outside. Some clients may have patios or lanais that they let their cats go out on for some fresh air, or they may even keep their cats out there most of the time. However, it is far more likely that you will run into an outdoor cat than an outdoor dog, especially in warmer climates. If your client has an outdoor cat, make sure to ask if the weather gets too hot or cold if they would prefer to have their cat inside in a particular room or area.

---

16. https://dogvacay.com

- Cats spend a good portion of each day sleeping, and are often more active at night. If the cat seems unusually lethargic or disoriented, this may signal a problem. Just like dogs, a bored or stressed cat will chew on items, knock over objects, and get into trash containers.

A cat's brain is more similar to a human's brain than that of a dog.[17]

- Cleaning out litter boxes is an obvious task for taking care of pretty much any cat. Depending on the number of cats your client has will determine if you need to clean it out multiple times per day or just in the morning and at night. Make sure you know where extra litter and supplies are kept. Note that cats are extremely sensitive and clean animals, so they may have an aversion to a dirty litter box and will use a corner of the carpet or a closet if they judge a litter box to be too dirty. Regular scooping of waste, and a complete change of litter, are necessary to prevent the cat from making a mess somewhere else.

17. www.animalleague.org

Bark Break!
Cats count on you

Cats, as I mentioned above, are incredibly sensitive to dirty environments and have an instinctual desire to be clean. Their cleanliness and happiness is directly dependent upon you as a sitter or as an owner.

For example, I once was a pet-sitter for a home that owned six indoor cats. They also had several fish in a large aquarium. I know what you're thinking, there must have been several litter boxes throughout the home and odor must have been an issue at times. However, this was not at all the case. You never would have known that this was a home that had any pets at all, if you ignored the kitty condos in the living room and the cat toys scattered in each room. The owners kept two large litter boxes in their laundry room and instructed me to clean them two to three times per day. Six cats produced quite a bit of waste, but since it was being taken out regularly and the box was being constantly topped off with more fresh litter, the laundry room smelled great and how it should—like clean laundry.

On the flip side, one of my childhood friends from elementary school owned just indoor two cats. Her family also kept two litter boxes in their laundry room. I never directly witnessed them taking care of old litter, but there was definitely a distinct odor near the laundry room pretty much at all times. I believe that the system of cleaning litter boxes at least twice a day should do the trick for most situations. There's no such thing as "too" clean!

- Cats typically require less food than dogs and do not really eat on a set schedule. Keeping a decent portion of food and plenty of water out at all times should do the trick, but this may vary by client.

- Some cats require either wet food or dry food, and some owners use a mixture to keep their cats happy.

- Make sure to ask your client if their cat requires any special medication or supplements.

- Cats may not be as rowdy as dogs, but they often enjoy a little playtime too. Make sure you know where toys and other supplies are kept. Keeping pets entertained while their owners are gone will make it more difficult for them to get into trouble.

Hamsters, Gerbils, and more

- Animals that live in cages or pens, such as hamsters, gerbils, guinea pigs, rats, ferrets, rabbits, hedgehogs, birds, etc. will all require similar care. If you take them out of their cage or pen to play with them, be careful where you do so. They may seize the opportunity for adventure if you give them too much freedom and can end up stuck in the Xbox. Or, even worse, they may have a Siberian Husky brother who may see them as a meal, not a playmate.

- While taking care of ferrets, rabbits, or larger mammals (you probably won't run into any raccoons though, but it could happen) make sure to take them out of their pen and give them room or space to roam around in for a while. Some may even want to play with you, but that depends on each pet's personality. Your client will already most likely have them in a room or safe space where it is OK to do so. It is also common to keep larger animals such as rabbits out on the patio or lanai. Be care if your client has a pool, though, but they will probably have a fenced area set-up for playtime.

Hamsters may run up to a mile a day.[18]

- Hamsters and other caged mammals will all require you to monitor their food bowl, water container, bedding cleanliness, and whether or not they need a treat or medicine. It is also likely that you may have to clean out their cage and replace it with fresh bedding if your client is gone for more than a few days.

- Hedgehogs are usually shy, nocturnal animals that can take some time to become used to being handled. They often spend much of the day sleeping and are active at night. Hedgehog owners often keep the animals in multi-level ferret or rabbit cages with an exercise wheel, toys, and an area to hide in, such as a box. Appropriate temperature is very important for hedgehogs. Make sure that your hedgehog's habitat is away from drafts, and keep the temperature between 68 and 80 degrees Fahrenheit.

 *Fish*

- Fish will probably be the easiest animal to care for—probably. You obviously cannot take a fish out of its tank and play with it, but that doesn't mean you can ignore it. Make sure to monitor the cleanliness of its tank or bowl, or, if your client has a filtered tank or large aquarium, that everything is running smoothly.

- There are three basic types of aquariums: saltwater, freshwater, and reef. Saltwater aquariums contain fish and other animals from ocean environments. Freshwater aquariums contain fish and plants from lakes, streams, and other freshwater sources. Reef aquariums, which may not contain any fish at all, will house other saltwater animals and plants such

---

18. www.petsintheclassroom.org

as coral, sea anemones, and mollusks. If you are not familiar with any of these, ask the client to provide you with detailed instructions.

- Be mindful of the portions of food or treats you feed clients' fish. Since you're dumping their meals directly into the water that they live and breathe in, it is easy to overdo it — which can end tragically.

- Tanks are usually equipped with a thermometer and a heater. You should check these every day to be sure the temperature remains within the client's stated normal range. Aquariums also have a water filter, usually one that bubbles so that oxygen is mixed into the water. During each visit, you should verify that these are working properly and rinse out the filter if it is becoming blocked. If the water becomes cloudy, or the walls become heavy with green or brown algae, you must clean the tank. Owners usually have a vacuum-like tool to siphon waste from the floor of the tank and algae from the walls. Be sure you know how to use these tools beforehand, and be careful not to suck up a fish along with the dirt.

- Since fish cannot come out and greet you when you enter a client's home, it may be easy to forget to feed them or check on them — especially if you are caring for multiple pets at the same home. It may be a good idea to set reminders on your phone or keep a checklist handy.

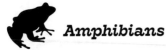 **Amphibians**

- Frogs and toads are colorful, popular pets that are easy to care for, and depending on the breed, active and entertaining. Frogs like Oriental fire-bellied toads have bright colors on their bellies, which are intended to scare away predators in the wild. Some frogs and toads secrete toxins, so it is wise to handle them as little as possible. If you must pick up a toad, wash your hands in clean water first and leave them wet. Never touch your eyes, mouth or face when you are handling an amphibian, and be sure to thoroughly wash your hands after.

- The type of food will depend on the breed, but most frogs eat insects and larva, so you will be handling insects if you take on a frog-sitting job. The client may feed the amphibians a specialized diet or may provide wax worms and crickets. Each amphibian should get two small wax worms or two small crickets per week. The larger frog breeds can eat whole live crickets, so be sure you understand your feeding responsibilities before you take the job. If you're squeamish about feeding live creatures to a pet, this may not be the client for you.

 ## Snakes, turtles, and other reptiles

- Whether or not you will have to take clients' snakes, turtles, tortoises, bearded dragons, frogs, lizards, salamanders, etc. out of their terrariums will depend on each pet or client. Again, if you do not feel comfortable taking care of a snake, for example, tell your client this to see if they can make other arrangements. Some of these animals may have a combination of a wet and dry living spaces. It is also likely that they will have some sort of heat lamp or warming device. Be mindful of these and whether or not they should remain on at all times.

- Food and fresh water should be available at all times for these animals, and they will probably eat throughout the day. Be mindful that snakes and bearded dragons may require or prefer live meals, such as rodents or crickets, respectively. However, it is also common for these animals to eat frozen meals, but they should be thawed before serving.

- Like mammals, it is important to make sure that reptiles are put back in their cages or terrariums and that lids or seals are closed properly, so they do not escape. Reptiles, especially snakes, are incredibly good at escaping even through the smallest spaces. It's also important to wash your hands thoroughly after handling reptiles as they often carry salmonella.

Birds

- Cockatiels, parrots, parakeets, and finches are some of the most popular birds for pet owners. Bird lovers enjoy their pets because of their beautiful songs, funny antics, and graceful behavior. Birds require a cage large enough to accommodate their wingspan, and the cage should offer a perch or two. Birds can be very sensitive to cold or drafts, so mind the temperature while the client is gone. Often, owners will provide a cloth to cover the bird, either to reduce distractions so the bird can sleep, or to cut down on drafts. Ask the bird owner about his or her practice when it comes to covering the cage.

- You may be asked to care for birds that are nesting eggs or have hatchlings. If so, you must take extra care not to disturb the nest or agitate the birds while cleaning and feeding. Make sure you understand any other special care requirements for the nesting brood before the owner leaves.

- Unless you're dealing with a particularly calm or gentle breed of bird, you probably won't have to take them out of their cage at all, and it's probably for the best if you don't. Still, make sure to monitor the cleanliness of their cage.

- Make sure to monitor their levels of food and water, and make sure you give them treats or any medicine, if necessary.

Other

I know what you're thinking, "What *other* pets?" However, there are people who own sugar gliders, chinchillas, monkeys, squirrels, pigs, crabs, ducks, chickens, owls, and other exotic varieties (if you can call a squirrel exotic). It is also very common for people to own livestock or larger mammals such as cows, sheep, goats, horses, and donkeys. If you know how to care for any of these *other* animals, then good for you! You probably have a good edge on the competition. If you do not, however, don't fear. It's likely that there are plenty of regular-old dog and cat owners in your area, and you'll have plenty of business.

In case you were wondering, here are a few tips about chinchilla care:

• Chinchillas are silky-soft rodents that look like a cross between a rabbit and a large mouse. They are playful, gentle, nocturnal animals that can be quite shy. They are most active in the evening and at night and can be very playful and rambunctious at these times. For this reason, you may want to schedule a pet-sitting visit for these creatures at night to take advantage of their playtime. They should be kept in a fairly quiet area during the day. Chinchillas require a lot of roughage, so the owner should provide a supply of good quality grass hay, along with pellets made for chinchillas. Ask the client to tell you the exact amounts of each type of food. Treats should be given in moderation (one teaspoon per day in total), and can include fruits (like fresh or dried apples, grapes, or raisins), carrots, celery, sunflower seeds, and rolled oats. The digestive system of chinchillas is fairly sensitive, so be careful with any drastic changes in diet.

In case you were wondering, here are a few tips about crab care:

• The most common type of pet crab is the hermit crab, which can be found in any shopping mall or pet store. They are low-maintenance pets that require little set-up, and can be easy for children to care for. Another popular pet is a fiddler crab, which has one very large front claw and one smaller one. These crabs need to live in a saltwater environment that also includes dry land. Fiddler crabs molt just as other crabs do. The owner will likely feed fiddler crabs fish or shrimp pellets.

Maintaining Relationships

Congratulations! You have some clients! Retention is just as important, if not more important, than taking on new clients. Seeking to provide quality care to the clients you already have will build your reputation on a strong foundation. Not that you're starting some huge corporation (but honestly, dream big, kid), but it is understood in the business world that it is usually five times more costly to attract a new customer than it is to keep an existing one[19]. This applies to you, too, in more ways than just money. Think about all of the effort and time it takes to not only meet with a potential client, but also figure out where they live, how to take care of their home and pets, and above all, actually secure their business. The more time you spend with your current clients, the better they will get to know you and will be able to do some legwork for you in terms of spreading the word about your awesome services.

---

19. (**www.invespcro.com**).

CASE STUDY:
REBEKAH SLONIM

How to Establish a Steady Pet-Sitting
Business — Even if the Dogs Aren't

One day, when my sister and I were about 11 or 12 years old, my mom came back on a summer evening from a chat with the neighbor, and she said, "Rachel and Rebekah, would you like to watch Dave and Sue's dogs while they go on vacation?"

Rachel and I — like many enterprising youngsters — had considered dog sitting before, and, while the job wasn't our own idea, we were delighted about the opportunity. We were just at the age when the notion of getting some kind of job and making some money seemed appealing.

For me, the summer had always been a time to read books as much as I could and spend some time every day playing outside, whether riding my bike in the subdivision or swinging on the swing set in the backyard. I was happy that this job wouldn't really interfere with that schedule — the neighbors lived only two doors down. Rachel and I just took our books over to Dave and Sue's for long leisurely summer afternoons of reading while petting the dogs and letting them out every now and then. They had a backyard, too, of course, and we would play with the dogs there — when we could convince them to play. They were older dogs that didn't need much activity and were far less energetic than our own dog, which was only a few years old at the time. They had to go down two steps to get to the patio outside, and often we had to gently nudge them up or down those steps.

We quickly established a routine. We went over to Dave and Sue's house three times a day — once in the morning, before the sun was completely up, to let the dogs out and feed them breakfast; once in the afternoon, for a long chunk of time, to pet them and give them attention as we read books and chatted; and once in the evening to feed them supper, let them out again, and encourage them to lie down and go to sleep.

The next year, Dave and Sue asked us to dog sit again, and they asked us the year after that, too. It became a predictable summer ritual. We would schedule our own vacations around Dave and Sue's so that we would be sure to be available.

Although fliers and business cards have their merit, especially at a job like pet-sitting, where you'll go into someone's house and take care of a treasured family pet, you're probably most likely to be hired if you know the owners personally. And you're most likely to keep getting hired if you always say yes. Your potential clients almost certainly find making arrangements for their pets stressful — especially if the pet wouldn't do well being kenneled and if that's not an option financially. If you are flexible enough to almost always say yes, do so! We were able to seamlessly fit not only Dave and Sue's schedule but also the dogs' routine into ours. Because we went over so often, the dogs grew attached to us — which only made the owners trust us more.

But even if the work is predictable, the dogs probably won't be. This past summer — several years after I had stopped dog sitting Dave and Sue's dogs — we dog sat for my husband's grandma for two weeks. Her young dog had separation anxiety and had many accidents, including one within thirty seconds of being let outside to go the bathroom!

Yet that didn't compare to what happened one summer afternoon, several summers after the first time that we dog sat Riley and Patchy.

That day, when we returned to our neighbors' house in the afternoon, Riley and Patchy were nowhere to be found. Generally, they scampered over to the garage door to greet us since we always came in through the garage. Or, they would be dozing in the living room, tails pounding on the couch once they realized we were coming.

We hunted through all the bedrooms in the house — territory we would never normally enter. A foul smell permeated the air in Dave and Sue's bedroom. There was Riley, and there was a huge pile of the foulest diarrhea I have ever smelled or am likely to ever smell. Occasionally, Patchy and Riley had pooped in the house before, but never like this. To further relay my point, I spent two summers working in a day care later on (changing many a poopy diaper) and none of the not-so-great smells topped this one! Rachel and I had never wanted to do anything less than clean up that diarrhea. We offered each other our half of the dog-sitting money — to no avail.

As both dogs began to alarmingly sniff the poo, we hustled them out of the room. Back in the living room, we brainstormed in despair about what to do. The smell was so bad that our eyes were watering, and by the time we picked up the phone to call our mom, we were crying with frustration.

After learning that we both had essentially refused to clean it up, she suggested that we ask our dad to help us — but reminded us that it might be fair to give him some of the money that we would earn. We offered our dad every cent that we were going to make. Guess what? He came home from work and cleaned up the diarrhea — and didn't make us pay him any money.

You might not have a benevolent dad on hand to clean up the mess for you, but you should be forewarned that dogs — somewhat like people — could always surprise you, even if you think they wouldn't behave in a certain way. Old age, separation anxiety, and just bad behavior can make your dog-sitting experience more exciting than you wanted it to be!

But, nevertheless, we always enjoyed our predictable routine of dog sitting with its unpredictable quirks.

Rebekah Slonim and her sister Rachel were pet sitters for their neighbors for nearly a decade until they moved away from their hometown of Columbus, Ohio.

Making your clients feel special

The easiest way to explain how to do this is pretty much this: each client is different and each pet is unique. So act like it. Take note of pet birthdays and send your clients a message or card on these days. If you really want to go above and beyond, deliver a bag of treats or a toy, too. If your client asks for updates on how their pet is doing, make sure to text or email them promptly. Unless you are told to do so, calling your clients will probably be too disruptive.

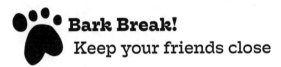 **Bark Break!**
Keep your friends close

There's an old saying, "Keep your friends close, but your enemies closer." This rings true in the business world as well, and even in the pet-sitting business, believe it or not. It is likely that you will attract a large percentage of your clients by being friends with them already, and by making friends with their friends. It's important not to ignore the second part of this phrase, too, as it is likely that some point in your life one of your enemies may become your friend. Not to mention, you should keep an eye on pet-sitters who may be in competition with you and may try to "steal" your business.

They may be in an important meeting if they are on a business trip or busy enjoying family time on vacation. Take a photo or two of their pet to keep them in the loop and in good spirits despite being separated. During your last visit, write a note or "report card" for each of their pets. If you're taking care of a fish, it hopefully won't get into too much trouble or excitement, but you never know. Your client will appreciate the sentiment and will probably love to hear if you did well taking care of their pet or pets and if they behaved.

 Cats "head-butt" people because they make them feel safe or they trust them.[20]

Quality control

Obviously if you have the ambition to start your own business at a young age, you have high standards for yourself. In any business environment, there will be tough competition. Even if there isn't another pet-sitter in town right now and you can run the game, that doesn't mean it won't change quickly. You can set your business apart by having the same high standards for your business as you do for yourself (after all, this shouldn't be difficult — you are the face of your business). Be mindful and take appropriate steps necessary to provide the absolute best care you can for all of your clients. It's a good idea to provide the option for your clients to give reviews or some sort of feedback for your services. Consider setting up a free survey through Google Docs or SurveyMonkey[21] and emailing them to your clients. This way, your clients will feel comfortable being honest about your services, and you will have a better idea of how you can improve in the future. Consider posting some of these reviews or insights on your Face-

---

20. www.viralforest.com
21. www.surveymonkey.com

book page or website, with permission from your clients. Potential customers will love to see recommendations or glowing reviews.

Business Policies

As a business owner, you will need to make general policies and procedures to ensure your business runs well.

General policies you will want to consider will include:

- **Your appointment hours:** Will you set specific parameters or will you be available whenever requested?

- **"Office" hours**: When can clients reach you, and how soon can they expect a reply to a message or email?

- **Handling payments:** When is payment required? Will clients have to pay a deposit beforehand and the balance when the work is completed? Will you have a grace or payment period? How will you handle late accounts or returned checks?

- **Pet Immunizations:** Will you require proof of immunizations and vet care before taking on a pet sitting engagement? Remember, if you are caring for multiple pets you could likely spread disease from one animal to another.

- **Non-sitting appointments:** Do you plan to charge for appointments when you are not providing animal care, such as an initial client interview or a key pick-up? Will you offer discounts if the client leaves a key with you?

- **Alternative sitters:** Will you share sitting responsibility with other sitters or provide a backup for an emergency? How will you handle multiple sitters taking care of the same pet or family members who share pet-sitting duties?

- **Pet identification:** Will you require all pets to wear an ID collar? What other ID methods will you expect?

- **Last-minute reservations:** Will you agree to take care of an animal at the last minute, even if it means that you will not be able to meet with the owner beforehand? Will you charge extra for these requests?

- **Holiday sitting:** Do you plan to charge more for appointments during the holiday or will you treat those as regular visits?

As your business progresses, you will likely find more issues for which you will need a policy. Remember that there is not just one way to run a sitting business; you will find what works for you and what you will need to manage closely.

In addition to outlining your business policies, it may also be wise to provide a friendly checklist for your clients before they leave their pets in your hands. You can give this to them when you pick up their keys or whenever you sign your agreement. Below is a sample checklist that you can use. By providing a checklist, it will make your job a lot easier and will ensure that you and your clients are on the same page.

Sample Client Checklist

Thank you for choosing (Your Business Name Here) for your pet-sitting needs. As your pet-sitter, I cherish the opportunity to be responsible for your pet's health and well-being. To ensure the best for your pet while you are gone, I have provided a checklist I recommend following. Do not hesitate to contact me if you have any questions or concerns!

☐ Provide documentation confirming that your pet is up-to-date on its shots. Make sure your pet wears current vaccination and ID tags on its collar, if applicable.

☐ If your pet likes to chew on things, set out its chew toys and whatever is necessary to protect your personal items and home furnishings from its teeth while you are away.

☐ Write out your pet's favorite hiding places. This helps the sitter find your pet if it does not immediately appear when the sitter arrives.

☐ If your pet has any unusual habits, like destructive behavior when left alone, change in bathroom habits or eating habits, etc., tell your sitter about these in advance.

☐ If you own multiple pets, please note that the sitter is aware and willing to care for all of your animals. Please do not ask the sitter to ignore a fish or an outdoor cat for a lower rate.

☐ Set out everything your pet needs in one visible and accessible area. This includes food, treats, utensils, food and water bowls, medications, leashes, can openers, toys, paper towels, cleaning supplies, garbage bags, litter and scoop, broom and dustpan and/or vacuum cleaner, pet towels, newspapers or other housebreaking materials, and a watering can for plants.

☐ Provide extra food, litter, and supplies just in case you return later than expected.

☐ Be sure to leave plastic bags for disposal of waste.

☐ Do not expect your sitter to pick up any pet messes that accumulated before their agreed period.

☐ Clean out your refrigerator so that food does not spoil, and wash all dishes so that there is no chance of ants or other pests invading the house.

☐ Make sure the sitter knows how to work your heat and air conditioner, fans, and other relevant lights and appliances. Make sure they are at a comfortable setting for your pet before you leave.

☐ Close off any areas of your home that are off limits to the pet or sitter, and let him or her know about it in advance. If there are any particular problems he or she should be aware of, such as a leaky faucet or a cat that likes to get into the garbage, tell him or her before you leave.

☐ If you are leaving anything specifically for your pet sitter, such as a batch of cookies or a tip, leave him or her a note. Sitters will not take anything from a house unless he or she is specifically invited to!

☐ If other people may access the house or care for the pets, make sure the sitter knows what he or she is responsible for and who he or she might encounter in the house. The sitter will not automatically know the difference between an authorized house visit and a break-in.

☐ Notify your veterinarian in writing that a pet-sitter will be caring for your pet and authorize the vet to extend medical care during your absence if it becomes necessary.

Below is sample veterinarian notification form that you can give your clients to fill out along with the checklist above.

Sample Veterinarian Notification

During my absence, a representative of our pet-sitting service will be caring for my animal(s) and has my permission to transport them to your office for treatment. I authorize you to treat my animal(s) and will be responsible for payment upon my return or will leave my credit card number below for you to charge.

Please file this notification with my records.

Client _____ Date _____

Animal(s) Names _____

Client signature _____

Credit card type _____

Credit card number _____ Expiration date _____

Following up

In addition to providing the opportunity for clients to give you valuable feedback, you can also follow up in other ways. Calling or meeting with your clients after they return so you can give them back their keys is a good foot in the door for not only payment (which you should be getting paid, after all!) but for setting up future visits. Using a master calendar or inputting events on your phone, computer, or planner would be a good way to keep track of when your clients are planning to go out of town or for trips they have already planned. This way, you can try to plan your schedule around theirs in order for you to provide future sitting services to them. However, make sure you take a vacation for yourself every once in a while. You'll be making bank as the best pet-sitter in town, after all!

Dealing With Difficult Clients

It's a harsh but true fact of life that not everyone you meet will like you, and, conversely, you won't like everyone you meet either. In any service industry profession, you are bound to encounter some very frustrating personalities that make you question why on earth you would ever enter into "X" business at all. Again, not trying to scare you. You're bound to be so overwhelmed with joy from the success stories of your business, satisfied clients, and happy, safe pets, that a few bad experiences may just kick you in the pants a little but will make you stronger in the end.

Since you are your own boss, you have the option to really do whatever you want. If a client (either a pet owner or the pet) is becoming more trouble than they are worth taking care of, you have the option to discontinue your services. This decision can arise due to a variety of factors or situations, but each case will probably be unique to you.

Every year, the Peruvian town of Churin holds a Guinea Pig festival, including an elaborate costume competition. [22]

Pesky pets

Just like people, some animals just won't like you. There's nothing wrong with that, but, as you can imagine, it will make your job as a pet-sitter that much more difficult. Some cats may hiss at you or scratch you if you attempt to come near them. They may attack you if you try to empty the litter box or rip your belongings to shreds. The best advice for dealing with pets like this is to just be aware at all times. If you become injured or can no longer deal with a troublesome cat, let your client know—you shouldn't feel at fault at all.

---

22. www.viralforest.com

Some dogs may bark uncontrollably at you, jump at you, or even nip at you. Some of these actions may be out of affection or excitement, but especially when dealing with larger breeds, it's important to be careful and cautious. If a dog you are taking care of becomes too aggressive or violent and you are unable to take care of them, do not continue to do so after notifying your client. In the meantime, have a parent or someone more experienced help you to care for troublesome animals.

Pesky people

Did you ever consider that people usually choose pets, not the other way around? Perhaps there's a reason for this. Pretty much everyone who owns a pet does so for the companionship—whether Mr. Whiskers likes it or not. Your clients may not have very good people skills, heck, they may be downright rude, but this doesn't mean that they are incapable of loving their animals or won't expect you to.

FUN FACT

More than 50 percent of pet owners surveyed would rather be alone on a desert island with their pet, not another person.[23]

If a client behaves too harshly to you (you'll know where the line is) or acts suspicious, discontinue service to them. If that seems too extreme but you still feel uncomfortable, have a parent, friend, or sibling accompany you on visits or even to client interviews. This is especially important to consider if they are a stranger and haven't been referred to you by a family member, friend, friend of a friend, or acquaintance.

---

23. www.animalleague.org

Keeping Safety in Mind

We have gone over a few things to look out for when visiting clients' homes or dealing with some of your customers and their pets. However, it is important to reiterate that if you ever feel unsafe, don't remain silent. Ask someone to accompany you on visits if you feel uncomfortable going to a particular neighborhood or home alone. If something is especially alarming, do not hesitate to call the police or someone who can help.

Whenever you reach a home, do a quick inspection of the outside before entering. If anything seems out of the ordinary or suspicious, don't enter if you're alone. Come back later when you can have the company of a parent, friend, or sibling. It may be wise to introduce yourself to neighbors. Not only will this allow you to chat with more potential clients, but also being familiar with them will help with your safety. They can help monitor your client's home when you're not there to take care of their pets.

What to do in emergency situations

Unfortunately, criminals are often aware of when people leave their homes or go on vacation. This makes pet-sitting a potentially dangerous job, especially if you are servicing a neighborhood unfamiliar to you. However, your clients know their home better than you do, and they likely wouldn't hire someone to come to their home if it is unsafe. If there is clear danger, call 911 promptly. It is far better for it to turn out to be nothing than for you to be in harm's way.

If a pet is acting particularly strange or out of the ordinary, or you know they have gotten sick, make sure to refer to the client profile for information on contacting the vet or animal hospital on record. Contact the pet's owner first. They may be aware of a certain condition or may just accredit sickness to nerves because they are absent. They should usually be able to determine if their pet is acting in a way that cannot be fixed with a little TLC, in which case you would have to act accordingly and professionally.

If you or a pet becomes injured, or the pet you're taking care of harms someone or something else, these are also situations for concern. It's important not to panic and to use your resources wisely. If no one is in immediate or life-threatening danger or has incredibly severe injuries, consult a neighbor or friend first. Visit a clinic or hospital after this step, if necessary.

Just because things can go wrong doesn't mean that they will, ever. It's better to be mentally prepared for emergency situations you'll never have to face than to become a pet-sitter expecting nothing but perfect days. Be confident, you've got this!

CHAPTER 4

Spreading the Word

It takes a brave soul to start a business from the ground up. Even if you have only taken care of your own pets or a few pets in your life, you're not out of luck in becoming a successful pet-sitter. Like all things, experience will come with time, patience, and dedication. An incredibly important aspect in ensuring the success of any business is plenty of exposure in its service area. We're talking about advertising, kids. Word of mouth from your happy customers will work wonders for you, but sometimes, if you have ambition to expand, you may need some extra help. This chapter will cover a variety of outlets for you to spread the word about your awesome services.

Advertising Tips

As you continue to secure clients, its important to keep in mind how much more you can handle. It's likely that you have classes, family responsibilities, and engagements in the community, or even another job — not to mention you should make time for a social life or downtime, too (don't try to grow up too fast, trust me). However, if you choose just one of the advertising options below, it'll help you keep clients throughout the year, even during seasons that aren't travel-heavy. That way, you'll also keep a steady flow of cash coming in.

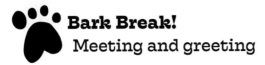

Bark Break!
Meeting and greeting

Like dogs, humans base their opinion of one another usually within the first few seconds of meeting. It's easy to see when and if two dogs are going to get along by quickly examining body language or even verbal cues.

If you're walking one dog, and another comes along that is wagging, has its ears floppy or back casually, its toes are poised, and its back is relaxed—this is definitely a dog destined to be a new friend. Let's call this dog number one. On the flip side, if a dog comes along that has its ears pinned to the side of its head, has its tail down, its dander up or has a rigid gait or posture—steer clear. Let's call this dog number two.

When meeting new people yourself, try to be like dog number one—friendly and approachable. Don't be afraid to smile, use appropriate eye contact, and use a firm handshake.

In order to effectively advertise, you have to think like your customers. As a pet-sitter, you'll probably be taking care of a lot of animals whose owners have a few kids. Advertise in areas where they'll be, such as:

- Little league or other sports facilities

- Parks or community centers

- Shopping centers

- Humane societies or local vets

- Clubs and non-profit organizations

- Travel agencies or real-estate offices

- Apartment and condominium complexes near you

- Nearby subdivisions or neighborhoods

Printed ads and fliers

This is perhaps the most traditional option, but not necessarily the easiest to keep up with. Simply draw up a design with your company name and logo, contact information, service area details, and anything else you'd like to include, such as sample prices. Canva[24] is a great online tool for designing all kinds of graphics, and it's free and easy to use. The site offers many pre-designed templates in a bunch of different layouts.

 Dogs will sneeze to tell other dogs that they're playing, and it won't turn into a fight even if they're being rough.[25]

It is recommended that you hand out printed ads in person so that potential clients can put a face to a name. Plus, you're guaranteeing that your customers actually hold your contact information in their hand, rather than it ending up in the trash. Some neighborhoods also have strict rules about leaving fliers and ads lying around, and you should keep this in mind. It may also be more cost effective if you have your fliers printed professionally, such as at an office supply or copy place. The quality will also likely be better, rather than using your mom's dinky printer she uses just for coupons.

---

24. www.canva.com
25. www.viralforest.com

A slight drawback to using printed ads is the notion of limited space. You can only fit so much information on a piece of paper—not to mention the cost of reprinting if there are mistakes.

Here is a sample flier generated using Canva:

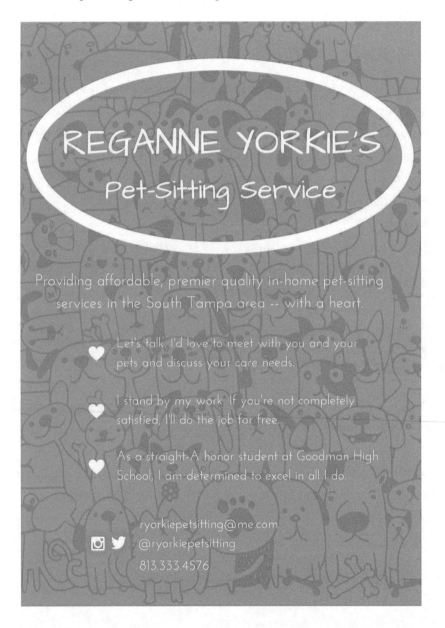

Digital ads and more

You don't need a ton of money to make effective advertisements. It's unlikely that you'll have enough dough or resources to run a television or radio ad, or even an ad on Google—for now. If you're friends with a local business owner who runs a website, or even if your church has a website, consider asking them if you can design a banner to advertise your services on their site. If your community has a local paper or magazine, reach out and inquire about advertising here—it may be way more affordable than you think.

Cold calling

If this sounds like a bit of an archaic practice, it kind of is, but that doesn't mean it can't work for you. Cold calling, by definition, is basically blindly calling people you don't know and seeing if they would be interested in doing business with you. This can work for you if you have some sort of directory for your neighborhood. You can also go really old school and use a phone book.

Cold calling isn't ideal, but it's another idea to consider. You may also consider reaching out to acquaintances by calling them to open the line of communication. This can be a good practice for rainy days when you can't get out in the community and advertise your business in person or hand out fliers—but it still has a personal effect.

Social Media

If you haven't caught on already, social media isn't just for creeping on your crush or sharing memes. It's incredibly easy to create another account for professional purposes—not to mention communicate with customers and post updates. You're probably already aware of many of these social media sites, but perhaps you haven't considered their potential for garnering new clients and business for you, not to mention presenting you as a competent, reliable, and wise choice for a pet-sitter within your community.

Bark Break!
Netiquette

I won't be the first or the last "adult" to consult you about your online posting habits or persona. Especially as a prospective business owner, and someone who is going to be welcomed into people's homes, you have an even more vital responsibility to present yourself as competent, mature, and sane. Plenty of young adults relish their youth and let it get the best of them — I'm not at all saying you can't act silly from time to time or have fun — just don't be one of those people who's compelled to tell the world about it. Delete buttons aren't a guarantee anymore, and you never know who's seen something you've thrown out there (or, worse, copied it or taken a screenshot of it).

It's pretty unlikely that you will be able to flawlessly separate your personal social media accounts from your business accounts, or your personal life from your "business" life, for that matter. Here's a good rule of thumb: if you wouldn't want the most judgy, opinionated person you know to see a photo of you or a blurb (regardless of whether you're connected on social media with them or not), don't post it. If you absolutely have to share something questionable, keep it private. Text your best friend about that raunchy meme, or send a snapchat to your sister with your snide caption about your least favorite professor. Your social media persona can be as colorful, funky, and fresh as you are — but it is also an important part of the foundation of your empire. Yes, you're building an empire.

Facebook

Instead of making a generic profile for your business, you can make a page that people (everyone, duh) can like, message, and post on. The general options are still obviously there, such as setting a spiffy cover photo and profile pic, posting updates and exciting promotions, as well as featuring some client reviews (with permission of course). You can also promote your business page from your personal profile, but make sure you don't have any sensitive content right next to your professional plug. Just because you had a fun night out doesn't mean your clients need to know about it.

Twitter

Creating a professional Twitter account is a great resource, even more so than Facebook in some ways, because you can follow current customers and potential customers without being perceived as creepy or intrusive (still be careful, though). Twitter, in general, is a much more public social media site than Instagram or Facebook. Users are much more likely to approve your follow requests or follow you back. Twitter still enables you to share updates and important information about your business. You can always share links to other sites as well. Twitter can be used to research potential clients more so than Facebook as well because it is slightly easier to locate and contact friends of friends or family of friends (or whatever) in a low-key setting.

Instagram

Instagram is a great way to share fun stories about the pets you care for, with permission from their owners. You can easily shed positive light on your valued clients and the great care that you provide. Posting pictures of happy pets and following people in your community will quickly build a stellar reputation for your business.

WordPress and other website resources

Running your own website, such as on WordPress, is a lot easier than it sounds. You can provide every ounce of information about your business anyone may ever want to know. Not to mention, WordPress offers completely free options.

Make sure to include:

- A brief bio about you

- A reliable email address

- Your availability and prices

- Customer reviews

- Photos and personal elements

- What specific services you offer and what pets you care for

- Your service area

- Links to your social media accounts

However, it may be more difficult for potential clients to find your website on their own. Make sure you provide the link to your website in the bio of your other social media sites and promote it often.

 Dachshund literally means "Badger Dog." They were originally bred to hunt and fight badgers in their burrows.[26]

---

26. www.viralforest.com

Other social media sites to consider

Besides the few popular sites that we have covered, it may be wise for you to set up a LinkedIn profile for yourself as well. If you have never heard of this site or think it's too soon for you to make one, it's not. It's basically Facebook for professionals.

You may also consider setting up a Snapchat account that you use for visits only; however, this can easily create issues. Only send "snaps" to relevant customers, and never give too many details about where your client lives. For example, if you're outside walking Cake, the yellow lab from down the street, just post a snap of Cake—not her owner's mailbox, street address, or anything too private. This may sound crazy because it's easy to regulate who you're friends with on Snapchat (and really any site, supposedly), but its better to be safe than sorry.

Email Marketing

Although email may not sound as exciting as social media, it is still an incredibly effective marketing tool. Why is it so effective? Well, practically everyone and definitely their mother has at least one email address. Email differs from social media in that consumers are typically more likely to be able to focus on one subject at a time. Scrolling through one's Facebook feed can get dull. *However,* banner ads on the side for weekend getaways in Montana, or a pet-sitter, for example, may still be easily ignored. Emails from businesses trying to attract you are both impersonal or generic and incredibly personal at the same time. After all, email messages come directly to your inbox and may have your name plugged into the subject line. However, their content may have reached a million other users.

Since emails can be easily deleted and forgotten, it is slightly less important to craft each one painstakingly. Time and attention should be instead spent on social media posts, which will usually linger a lot longer and require more customer interaction. Clean, attractive emails with one or two graphics and a link to your website or contact information can be just as effective as bedazzled, meme-ridden ones, if not more so.

How exactly can I get into email marketing?

It's not nearly as complicated as it sounds. Once you have compiled a decent list of interested clients, you can create emails to send directly to all of them at once. This can include promotions you are running, an update on your availability, or just a friendly hello. There are free services such as MailChimp[27] where you can create attractive, informative emails and send them to whomever you please. MailChimp also offers software that tracks if your email has been opened and if any links or resources have been clicked on.

What should I be emailing my clients?

You can email your clients pretty much anything you would post on social media. That's the beauty of owning your own business; you call all of the shots. Below are a few examples of content to include in a few different types of emails/situations.

If you are pursuing a new client . . .

Think friendly introduction. It may be the first time they are hearing of your business, or they may have forgotten that they heard about your business from a friend. You don't want to come off as annoying or too aggressive, as they may shy away or mark you as "SPAM" you or as "junk" — and

---

27. www.mailchimp.com

you aren't junk. If you use an email marketing service such as MailChimp, there are links where your clients can unsubscribe themselves.

> **Subject line:** Are you a proud pet owner in need of a caring, reliable pet-sitter?
>
> **Body:**
>
> Hi there,
>
> My name is Carlos Tamland, founder of Carlos Cares Pet-Sitting Services. I am also an honor student at West Catalina High School. If you are living in the northern San Diego area and are looking for an affordable, conscientious pet-sitting professional, I would love to offer my services to you.

Now that whoever is reading your email has an idea of who you are and, bluntly, what you want, you can go into further detail about why they should respond to your email, visit your website, or contact you for more information. You can include feedback from happy customers (with permission), a photo or two of some of the pets that you care for (with permission), or a list of specific services that you offer. Don't feel the need to inundate them with every ounce of information—it's good to leave them with a question or two so they are more likely to reach out to you directly.

> **Body (cont.):**
>
> I have experience caring for a wide variety of animals, from dogs of all shapes and sizes, to cats, to hamsters, to turtles and snakes, to rabbits, fish, and more.
>
> My passion for animal care inspired me to create a pet-sitting service, and I will hopefully be who you choose the next time you need someone to care for your pets due to a business trip, day trip, or family vacation. Whatever the case may be, I would love to meet you and your pet or pets!

"Carlos treated my dog Snookie as if she was his own. It was great having him visit my home so that Snookie could feel more comfortable while I was out of town. Carlos is the absolute best!" – Janet Edmonds, valued client

A few additional services I offer include:

- Grooming
- Overnight pet-sitting
- Light housecleaning
- "Kennel" services — your pet can stay with me at my pet-friendly home so they are never alone while you're gone!

Now that your potential client knows a little bit more about you, the closing section should reiterate all of your contact information and your willingness/want to sign them as a client.

I appreciate you taking the time out of your day to read a little bit about Carlos Cares Pet-Sitting Services. I would love to speak with you more or schedule a client interview. Please respond to this email or see other methods of contacting me at the end of this email.

You can also visit my website at carloscarespetsitting.wordpress. com or find my business page on Facebook.

I look forward to hearing from you!

Only the best for pets,
Carlos

(597) 321-4412
carloscarespetsitting@gmail.com

If you are updating an existing client . . .

Again, think friendly and inviting. People can't help it if they haven't needed a pet-sitter in a while and thus haven't contacted you. Maybe you'd like to mention that you are discounting your services for the month of February.

Subject line: Furry Friends and Family February Promotion

Body:

Dear valued client,

As a customer of Carlos Cares Pet-Sitting Services, I feel that you and your pets are family. As a special thank you for your business and support, I would like to offer you 30 percent off my pet-sitting services for the month of February.

So, go ahead, plan that family trip to the beach or the mountains. I'll gladly take care of your pet(s) — it's truly my pleasure.

Only the best for pets,
Carlos

(597) 321-4412
carloscarespetsitting@gmail.com

CHAPTER 5

Expanding Your Business

How to Track Your Success

We've discussed in this book a few times the importance of keeping accurate, detailed profiles of all your clients and experiences. Make it a habit to go over everything you have gathered and learned every few months. This way, you can not only see how you've grown personally and professionally, but you can also gauge where you can focus your energy next. Maybe there is a new subdivision a mile away that you would like to start advertising in. Maybe you now feel comfortable taking care of birds or have gained experience grooming dogs, and you'd like to add that to your list of services.

Keeping records

Besides keeping paper records and digital copies, it may be wise to keep a journal of your experiences as a pet-sitter as well. This can be done using a note app on your phone, or, if you're more old-fashioned, using a hearty ol' notebook. Taking time to review how your business is coming along will be of great benefit to you. Sometimes, lessons you learn don't become apparent until months down the road with some personal reflection.

 Cats can sleep up to 16 hours in a day.[28]

How to Know if You're Ready for More

There's not one solid answer to this question—you're ultimately the decision-maker, and you know yourself better than anyone. Expanding may seem like a daunting task, but, like anything, can become incredibly manageable if you break it down into smaller parts.

Where do you even begin?

Start by again mapping out your availability, especially if it has recently changed. Maybe you're in the summer semester of school, and you're taking time off from classes so you have more free time. Or, maybe your schedule has just changed in general and you have different availability.

Take on a few new clients at a time; don't overload yourself.

---

28. www.animalplanet.com

Bark Break!
Ten tips to have a better day

1. Set an alarm for at least five minutes before you really need to be up. If you're prone to snoozing—make a conscious effort not to for an entire week and see how you feel. If you give yourself more time in the morning to wake up and get prepared for your day, it will benefit you more than five or 10 extra minutes of sleep ever will.

2. Eat breakfast. If you're one of those people who don't like breakfast food (first of all, how can you not?), eat something you do like instead. Make sure to start your day with a balanced mixture of protein, some carbs, and a dash of good fat. For example, this can be an egg white omelet with a sprinkle of shredded cheese and a piece of grainy toast with some nut butter. Fruits and vegetables are great in the morning, too (or at any time throughout the day).

3. If you're already nervous or worrying about something, stop. Think about the last thing that you were nervous or worried about. It went probably went OK, maybe even great, and you're still standing. Don't let the thought of something knock you down before you even try.

4. Wear clothing, shoes, and accessories that make you feel good. Look good; feel good—it's as simple as that.

5. Give someone a compliment. This can be a random person on the bus, your mom or dad, or one of your friends. If

anything, text or email someone that you're thinking of them or that you hope they have a good day. Sharing kind words with others is an easy way to create happiness for you, even at your gloomiest.

6. Make a physical list. This can be in a notebook or on your phone, and it doesn't need to be extensive or overly complicated. There's something incredibly satisfying about deleting or crossing off tasks as the day goes on. Not making any check marks or deletions? Don't worry. Get back out there tomorrow.

7. Listen to a few of your favorite songs. Taking a few moments to yourself to listen to music can help set you in the right mood before taking on any task.

8. Get some exercise. Instead of taking the bus to class, try walking instead. Going to the gym in the morning is also a great way to wake yourself up, depending on the intensity of your workout. Gym sessions can also be great throughout the day or in the evening to blow off steam.

9. Stay hydrated. Yes, I'm just another annoying mom if you haven't realized already. Dehydration is linked to so many different health complications, not to mention it is far easier to get a headache or upset stomach without enough water in your system.

10. Pet a dog. Or a cat. Or a hamster. Or a turtle. Watch a squirrel do squirrel things for a few minutes. It's a good way to get your mind off of things that may be bothering you or give you renewed perspective.

To make expansion work properly, it will take quite a bit of planning because you're essentially reformatting your business. You should evaluate your visits not only in terms of time but also spatially. In other words, try not to plan visits several miles away from one another during rush hour—unless you absolutely have to.

Possible Expansion Ideas

We live in a highly consumerist society. If you want a certain product or a certain service, there are most likely a variety of people willing to meet your needs. As a pet professional, you are not at all limited to what you can offer. If a person can buy it for themselves—think luxury shampoos, gourmet baked goods, custom clothing, stickers, water bottles, toys, etc.—they're probably willing to purchase it for their pets as well. Below are a few ways you can expand your services to not just include the standard sitting activities.

Pet grooming

As your skills and experience increase, you may want to offer in-home pet grooming to your clients. Depending on the species and breed, grooming could include bathing the pet, brushing and clipping its coat, clipping nails, teeth, or wings, removing tear stains from fur, cutting out matted fur (or dreads on those cool mop dogs, Komondors), flea and tick removal, or treating the animal's skin. Pet grooming requires special tools such as clippers, scissors, various brushes, nail trimmers, and special shampoos and ointments.

Providing in-home grooming is different than providing services at a grooming store. You will need to take your tools with you and adapt to the conditions in the home. Some mobile groomers have a van completely outfitted to roll up the client's driveway and perform grooming from the van. As you can imagine, this requires a considerable outlay of money, but if you've got it, go for it! You can even go as far as Harry Dunne in *Dumb & Dumber* and turn your vehicle into a sheepdog.

When grooming the animals, it is important to pay attention to the disinfecting of tools and the grooming area. If you treat animals for fleas or mites, be sure that you're not spreading that to the next animal on your sitting schedule. As with every pet-sitting appointment, wash your hands thoroughly with antibacterial soap before caring for the next animal.

Sitters should complete professional grooming training or gain experience by working in a pet grooming facility before offering grooming services. There are a few resources in the back of this book for breed grooming certification; these organizations can also provide guidance on how to charge appropriately for your services.

Pet products

Some pet-sitters also promote and sell products specific to the pets in which they specialize. This could include specialized diets or meal supplements, leashes, toys, pet clothing, water bottles, or hygiene products. If you want to sell products, be sure that you have room in your home for an inventory. Ask friends, family, and clients if they have any products in mind. Price your products so that you will make enough profit to benefit your business. If you're buying custom products in bulk, it will obviously be cheaper, but don't go so crazy that you waste money on items that will just collect dust in the attic. You can also give away these products as promotional items or on pets' birthdays.

People are spending more money on their pets than ever. Many hobbies or outside interests, such as painting, scrapbooking, or sewing, can help you offer additional services or products to pet lovers. If you enjoy painting, offer portraits of your clients' pets for sale. If you like to scrapbook, sell scrapbooks of images your clients provide of their pets. If you enjoy sewing or embroidering, make custom blankets, towels, and more.

 In 2016, more than $66 billion was spent on pets in the U.S. alone.[29]

Pet bakery

Just like people, pets love to eat You can easily set yourself apart by offering homemade treats for your customers. Natural varieties in stores are often expensive, but treats made at home in bulk don't cost that much to produce. If you're someone who likes to bake, you can make simple homemade treats and even personalize them with a stamp of your business logo or pet-friendly "icing."

---

29. www.americanpetproducts.com

Here are a few recipes you can try:

Homemade Dog Biscuits

1 tbsp. (or 1 package) dry yeast

3-½ cups lukewarm chicken or
   meat broth

3-½ cups unbleached flower

2 cups whole-wheat flour

1-cup cornmeal

½ cup skim milk powder

1 egg

Preheat oven to 300°F. Dissolve the yeast in the lukewarm chicken or meat broth. Let the yeast broth mixture set 10 min. Mix together the flours and cornmeal and pour into the yeast mixture. Roll the resulting dough out ¼" thick. Cut desired shapes from dough.

Mix together skim milk powder and egg. Brush biscuits with egg wash. Bake on greased cookie sheets for 45 min. Turn oven off and leave biscuits in overnight to finish hardening. Yields approx. 5-dozen medium-sized biscuits.

Kitten Cookies

1-cup whole-wheat flour

¼ cup soy flour

1 tsp. catnip

1 egg

1/3 cup skim milk

2 tbsp. wheat germ

1/3 cup powdered milk

1 tbsp. unsulfured molasses

2 tbsp. butter, vegetable oil, or
   canola oil

Preheat oven to 350°F. Mix dry ingredients together. Add molasses, egg, oil, and milk. Roll out flat onto greased cookie sheet and cut into small, cat bite-sized pieces. Bake for 20 min. Let cool and store in tightly sealed container.

Homemade Bird Balls

1 lb. lard   6 cups oats

1 jar of peanut butter   2 cups sunflower seeds

5 cups cornmeal   2 cups raisins

Mix all ingredients together. Roll into about 5 or 6 small balls. Roll balls in a few additional sunflower seeds and raisins. Place the balls in a bird feeder or a bird's food dish. Note: these also make delicious treats for wild birds. Just place the treat on a feeder, deck rail, or in a suet feeder.

Keeping You and Your Business Thriving

Your business is doing really well. You have a ton of happy clients and a few new ones contact you often—you love your job and you hope you can support yourself on pet-sitting alone for the rest of your days. Not to get all dark and twisty on you, but the universe is perpetually susceptible to change. Things are constantly falling apart — but don't fear. There is a way to keep yourself jivin' and thrivin' as long as you're in this business.

How to avoid burnout

Put simply, running your business is a task like any other—like algebra homework, for example. What do you do when you get tired of logarithms or simplifying variable equations? You take a break. You should do the same every once in a while with your business. If it becomes impossible for you to clear your schedule of all clients at any given time (good for you!), then refer your clients to another pet-sitter for the time being, have a friend or family member fill in for you, or explain to them that you really need a few weeks to yourself. When you return, you'll be as fresh as a daisy and ready to take on the world (or the neighborhood) once more.

Burnout is unfortunately a very common fact of life that you will experience many, many times. How easily you bounce back says a lot about you as an individual. Depending on the situation, it may be easier or more difficult for you to get the pep back in yo' step. One of the most effective ways to re-energize yourself for any task or job is to simply walk away for a period of time. Of course, you shouldn't do so irresponsibly, and you should notify your clients that you are taking some personal time.

 People spend an average of almost three hours per day doing some sort of leisure activity in the U.S.[30]

For some people, it takes them a good 48-72 hours to truly relax or unwind from pressure that they may be putting on themselves (or that may be put on them) on the daily. Some people may require more time, and that's OK. Take breaks while you're young and still have plenty of people around to count on and help you out—planning and successfully taking vacation days doesn't get easier for the majority of busy professionals later in life.

Plan a weekend beach trip with your friends, go to a theme park, or just let your hair down and lounge around at home for a few days. Make sure that you have put everything work-related away and out of reach. This is important YOU time. When you return, it may still be difficult to be excited about your job again. But, remember, this is the pet-sitting business, not an accounting firm. You chose a fun profession and it should feel like such, but, yet again, there's nothing wrong with dreaming of being an accountant either.

---

30. www.bls.gov

Building a foundation for the future

It's important to capitalize on your ambitions and explore your passions while you're young. Putting yourself out there is the absolute best way to learn more about how you operate—your strengths, your weaknesses, your hidden talents—all of which cannot be easily realized unless you test yourself. You may not want to be a pet-sitter for the rest of your days, and that's totally understandable. However, the interpersonal and business skills that you acquire from starting and running your own business are invaluable and can be translated into any industry. A knack for relating to people or being well-versed in customer service will bode well for you for all of your future business encounters and will easily make you the go-to guy or gal.

Already a business owner, you can sell yourself based off of tips and tools you've learned about in this book—dealing with clients, advertising, using social media, taking care of finances, etc.

The older you get, the more you'll hear about developing "marketable skills," or some variation of this concept. Be among the first and few in the crowd of youngins at job fairs in your town, college, or university that knows what these are and what you can boldly bring to any company's table.

Conclusion

Congratulations! You've made it through the entire guide to pet-sitting. Hopefully you're feeling more confident and excited than ever to go take care of pets that need you. As a pet-sitter, you have been granted a unique opportunity to improve the lives of the pets and owners who use your services—so treat this opportunity like a privilege. You may succeed at times and fail at others, and it may not be all fun work. The absolute worst thing you can do is let failure stop you from moving forward or live in fear of "screwing up." You are not defined by your mistakes; you are defined by how you carry yourself through them. It will be hard for anyone you come into contact with to not gain respect for you if you always take ownership.

In many ways, this is not only the beginning of your journey as a pet-sitter, but also presumably the beginning of your journey as a business professional. There is great pride that comes along with making your own money and paying your own way, even if it's just a little bit at a time. Let your love of pets and enthusiasm for great care pull you onward and upward—you've got this.

Bibliography

"Cat Facts You Won't Believe!" *Animal Planet*. 29 July 2016. Web. 27 Dec. 2016.

"Cool Pet Facts." *North Shore Animal League America*. Web. 27 Dec. 2016.

Ford, Allison. "23 of the Weirdest Facts About Cats and Dogs." **More. com**. More, 09 Nov. 2016. Web. 27 Dec. 2016.

"Fun Facts about Animals." *Pets In The Classroom*. Web. 27 Dec. 2016.

Golon, Caroline. "25 Cool Dog Facts." *Petfinder*. Web. 27 Dec. 2016.

"Interesting Facts About Dogs." *MSPCA*. Angell, Web. 27 Dec. 2016.

"McLendon, Russell. "36 Random Animal Facts That May Surprise You." *MNN - Mother Nature Network*. 31 Mar. 2016. Web. 27 Dec. 2016.

Most Popular Dog Breeds in America." *American Kennel Club*. Web. 27 Dec. 2016.

"Pet Statistics." *ASPCA*. Web. 27 Dec. 2016.

"The 24 Most Adorable Animal Facts . . . OF ALL TIME." *Viral Forest*. 13 Jan. 2015. Web. 27 Dec. 2016.

Glossary

Accreditation program: A program that grants evidence of expertise or knowledge in a certain subject area.

Advertising: A method of promoting awareness to attract business or sales for a product or service. A company may do so digitally, in print, on the radio or television, etc.

Azalea: A deciduous flowering shrub of the heath family with clusters of brightly colored, sometimes fragrant flowers. Technically classified as rhododendrons, azaleas are characteristically smaller than most other rhododendrons.

Burnout: Phenomenon that can occur after performing mental or physical work for an extended period of time. May include feelings of exhaustion, fatigue, or disinterest in subject matter.

Capacity: The ability or power to do, experience, or understand something.

Checking account: An account at a bank against from which the account depositor can write checks.

Clowder: A group of cats.

Cloud-based: A term that refers to applications, services or resources made available to users on demand via the internet from a cloud computing provider's servers.

Cold calling: To make an unsolicited call on (someone), by telephone or in person, in an attempt to sell goods or services.

Debit card: A card issued by a bank allowing the holder to transfer money electronically to another bank account when making a purchase.

Dependable: Trustworthy or reliable.

Effective: How influential something is, such as advertisement.

Empire: An extensive operation or sphere of activity controlled by one person or group.

Expansion: The act of increasing, as in influence or exposure.

Exposure: How much attention a subject receives or is given, or how much is known about a subject already.

Generic: Commonplace or not special.

Grooming: A service for animals that includes bathing, brushing, trimming or shaving hair or fur, nail clipping, and often blow-drying.

Humane society: This is a group that aims to stop human or animal suffering due to cruelty or other reasons. In many countries, humane societies are now used mostly for the prevention of cruelty to animals.

Identification: May refer to special tag or indicator to notify the identity of a person or pet.

Immunization: Process by which an animal or human is made immune or resistant to an infectious disease, typically by the administration of a vaccine.

Initial expenses: Money spent when to allow a business to develop or become established.

Invoice: A list of goods sent or services provided, with a statement of the sum due for these; a bill.

Irony: A state of affairs or an event that seems deliberately contrary to what one expects and is often amusing as a result; usually humorous.

Kindle: A group of kittens.

Lactose Intolerant: The inability to digest lactose, a component of milk and some other dairy products. The basis for lactose intolerance is the lack of an enzyme called lactase in the small intestine. The most common symptoms of lactose intolerance are diarrhea, bloating, and gas.

Logo: A graphic, symbol, collection of words, or any combination of the three to represent a business or organization.

Manageability: How easy is it is to work with someone or something.

Mission Statement: Longer-term goals or that an individual or organization strives toward or statements or values that they abide by.

Netiquette: The correct or acceptable way of communicating on the internet.

Obedience School: School that dogs can attend and receive a diploma from upon completion. Skills taught include overall proper behavior, common verbal commands, and how to sit and heel.

Objectives: Statements or shorter-term goals that outline how someone or something operates.

Operational expenses: Money spent to allow a business to run properly or smoothly.

Pandemonium: A group of parrots.

Permission: Allowing something, such as an action or motion, to occur.

Personal brand: Someone's appearance, reputation, logo, persona, etc. It is everything that encompasses a professional.

Pet Sitters International (PSI): An organization that offers an education program and accreditation for completed coursework related to pet-sitting.

Professional: Being skilled or competent in a particular manner or area.

Profit: A financial gain, especially the difference between the amount earned and the amount spent in buying, operating, or producing something.

Promotion: A sale or discount campaign that a business may offer.

Proverb: a short pithy saying in general use, stating a general truth or piece of advice.

Quirk: A peculiar behavioral habit.

Rambunctious: Full of energy, crazy.

Retention: A business' ability to keep clients.

Savvy: Well versed in a subject matter.

Screenshot: An image of the data displayed on the screen of a computer or mobile device.

Self-evaluation: Manner of writing a review of oneself over a given period of time to examine goals or growth.

Self-sufficient: Emotionally and intellectually dependent, needing no outside help in satisfying one's basic needs.

Service area: Region in which a business offers its services.

Service kit: Everything that must be packed in order for you to have a successful or enjoyable day on the job.

Specialize: A specific area of expertise one offers or has knowledge about.

Subdivision: A section or area a neighborhood that may have its own name and security.

Suet: The hard fatty tissue about the loins and kidneys of beef, sheep, etc., used in cooking or processed to yield tallow. It is a high-energy treat that attracts insect-eating birds in the wild or can also be used to feed pet birds.

Survey: A questionnaire businesses, organizations, or individuals use to gather feedback and data.

Workload: The amount of time or number of different tasks a person is responsible for over a given period.

Veterinarian: A person qualified to treat diseased or injured animals.

Appendix

Sample Client Checklist

Thank you for choosing (Your Business Name Here) for your pet-sitting needs. As your pet-sitter, I cherish the opportunity to be responsible for your pet's health and well-being. To ensure the best for your pet while you are gone, I have provided a checklist I recommend following. Do not hesitate to contact me if you have any questions or concerns!

☐ Provide documentation confirming that your pet is up-to-date on its shots. Make sure your pet wears current vaccination and ID tags on its collar, if applicable.

☐ If your pet likes to chew on things, set out its chew toys and whatever is necessary to protect your personal items and home furnishings from its teeth while you are away.

☐ Write out your pet's favorite hiding places. This helps the sitter find your pet if it does not immediately appear when the sitter arrives.

☐ If your pet has any unusual habits, like destructive behavior when left alone, change in bathroom habits or eating habits, etc., tell your sitter about these in advance.

☐ If you own multiple pets, please note that the sitter is aware and willing to care for all of your animals. Please do not ask the sitter to ignore a fish or an outdoor cat for a lower rate.

☐ Set out everything your pet needs in one visible and accessible area. This includes food, treats, utensils, food and water bowls, medications, leashes, can openers, toys, paper towels, cleaning supplies, garbage bags, litter and scoop, broom and dustpan and/or vacuum cleaner, pet towels, newspapers or other housebreaking materials, and a watering can for plants.

☐ Provide extra food, litter, and supplies just in case you return later than expected.

☐ Be sure to leave plastic bags for disposal of waste.

☐ Do not expect your sitter to pick up any pet messes that accumulated before their agreement period.

☐ Clean out your refrigerator so that food does not spoil, and wash all dishes so that there is no chance of ants or other pests invading the house.

☐ Make sure the sitter knows how to work your heat and air conditioner, fans, and other relevant lights and appliances. Make sure they are at a comfortable setting for your pet before you leave.

☐ Close off any areas of your home that are off limits to the pet or sitter, and let him or her know about it in advance. If there are any particular problems he or she should be aware of, such as a leaky faucet or a cat that likes to get into the garbage, tell him or her before you leave.

☐ If you are leaving anything specifically for your pet sitter, such as a batch of cookies or a tip, leave him or her a note. Sitters will not take anything from a house unless he or she is specifically invited to!

☐ If other people may access the house or care for the pets, make sure the sitter knows what he or she is responsible for and who he or she might encounter in the house. The sitter will not automatically know the difference between an authorized house visit and a break-in.

☐ Notify your veterinarian in writing that a pet-sitter will be caring for your pet and authorize the vet to extend medical care during your absence if it becomes necessary.

Sample Veterinarian Notification

During my absence, a representative of our pet-sitting service will be caring for my animal(s) and has my permission to transport them to your office for treatment. I authorize you to treat my animal(s) and will be responsible for payment upon my return or will leave my credit card number below for you to charge.

Please file this notification with my records.

Client _____ Date _____

Animal(s) Names _____

Client signature _____

Credit card type _____

Credit card number _____ Expiration date _____

Sample Business Plan Outline

1. Business summary

   a. Objectives

   b. Mission statements

   c. Keys to success

2. Management summary

   a. Goals as your own boss

   b. Terms for your assistants (if applicable)

3. Products and services

   a. Product and service descriptions

   b. Technology you will use

   c. Future products and services

4. Check out the competition

5. Service area

   a. Area needs

   b. Future growth

6. Strategy for services

   a. Competitive edge

   b. Marketing/Promotional strategy

      i. Social Media

7. Establishing price

   a. Initial costs

   b. Operational costs

   c. What you will charge

Sample Business Plan: Reganne Yorkie's Pet-Sitting Service

1. Business summary

As an aspiring pet-sitting professional and founder of Reganne Yorkie's Pet-Sitting Service, there is nothing I won't do to ensure the happiness and health of the pets I care for. I seek to provide affordable, premier quality services for pets in the South Tampa area. This will include traditional pet-sitting services, grooming, and homemade treats.

a. Objectives

Through attention to detail, patience, and enthusiasm, I plan to build a reliable client base and reputation. I would like to work for at least five new clients within the next five months, and continue offering my services to my family and friends.

b. Mission statements

To be recognized as a positive role model in my community and a trustworthy, caring pet-sitter.

To remain calm, cool, and collected, even when tasks are difficult.

To eventually expand my services to provide care to more clients at a time over a larger region, without compromising quality.

c. Keys to success

My keys to success include: a positive attitude, treating my clients like family, attention to detail, organization, and dedication.

2. Management summary

a. Goals as your own boss

As my own boss, I will uphold very high standards for myself and will always do my best to accommodate all of my clients. If any issues arise, I will handle them calmly and strategically. I will carry myself professionally and I will be responsible with my time. If business goes as well as planned, I will reward myself with time off intermittently, or, eventually, that new car I've been looking at.

b. Terms for your assistants

When she is available, my sister will act as my assistant. I will pay her 40 percent of every job she assists me with, and 90 percent for any job she takes on for me if I am unavailable. I will hold her to the same high standards I hold myself, and she understands that she is my employee.

If at any time anyone else helps me for an extended period, I will also offer him or her a cut.

3. Products and services

   a. Product and service descriptions

   I plan to not only offer traditional pet-sitting services, but also grooming and homemade treats. My standard pet-sitting services will include dog walking, mess cleanup, watering of houseplants, taking care of the mail and newspapers, and other requests within reason. I will inform clients of my grooming experience as a volunteer at a pet hospital this past summer. Grooming services will include bathing, nail clipping, and trimming. The homemade treats I provide will be all natural, and I will make sure to ask my client's if their pet has any allergies.

   b. Technology you will use

   I will mainly use my phone for my business but I will back up important client information on Dropbox so I can access it from my laptop as well. I will use reminders, notes, and other scheduling apps to keep me organized and back up everything to the cloud. I will set up a Twitter, Facebook, Instagram, and WordPress accounts for Reganne Yorkie's Pet-Sitting Service. I will use my cell number as a method of contacting me.

   c. Future products and services

   I would like to eventually provide more varieties of homemade treats as well as be a go-to expert in pet grooming. Certain breeds or individual pets require more expertise and higher-quality tools. I hope to be able to offer this in the future.

4. Check out the competition

5. Service area

My service area will include residences in or near South Tampa. I will be able to use a car, so expansion outside of this area may eventually be feasible.

a. Area needs

I recognized a need in my neighborhood for a reliable, quality pet-sitter because a lot of families own pets and travel often. By allowing pets to remain in their homes, this will improve the comfort level for them while their owners are away. Since I am serving my own community, I have already become acquainted with many pets, and many dogs are friendly with my dog, Copper.

b. Future growth

I hope to eventually expand to be able to serve other areas within Tampa. However, if it becomes too difficult for me to provide the quality of care my clients deserve, I will continue to focus on just South Tampa. I can instead try to gain every client possible within my neighborhood and expand internally, versus externally.

6. Strategy for services

a. Competitive edge

I will have an edge on the competition because my services will be more thorough, affordable, and available. I have heard of a few people offering pet-sitting services in my area, but nothing official. However, I plan to make a legitimate business out of it. There are luxury pet spas and resorts around, but many of them require booking months in advance and they cannot focus on the pets they care for as easily due to their higher volume. I can offer every pet the care, love, and attention it de-

serves for a modest price. I am also set apart from some of my competitors because I offer homemade treats and grooming services.

b. Marketing/Promotional strategy

Since I am already very skilled and consumed by social media most of the time, I will devote most of my energy to successfully promoting my business. I will allow myself to use my personal accounts now and then, but I believe it is important to be thorough and follow through with all interactions and interest in my business.

i. Social Media

I will use Twitter, Facebook, Instagram, and WordPress to spread the word about my business. If necessary, I will ask my church if I can buy an ad in the weekly bulletin, as I believe this would be a good way to get clientele in different neighborhoods than mine but that are still within reasonable distance.

7. Establishing price

a. Initial costs

Initially, I will invest $150 in my business for various supplies. I will buy a new backpack to use exclusively for my pet-sitting jobs, a binder, a small dog toy and leash, a large dog toy and leash, a cat toy, and supplies to make homemade treats.

b. Operational costs

Different costs that I expect to incur while my business is up and running include filling up my car with gas, servicing my car, replacing other supplies I have purchased if needed, and buying supplies to make more homemade treats. I may also choose to purchase an ad in my church's bulletin. I do not expect these costs to exceed $200 per month.

c. What you will charge

I will charge $12 per "Pet Plus" visitation and $6 per "Pet Standard" or light visitation. "Pet Plus" visitations are usually an hour long and include a 30-minute dog walk or 30-minutes of playtime with other animals. Either plan includes one pet and each additional pet will be $3-$6 extra. All fish care is free. "Pet Plus" visitations also include check-ups on the owner's home, taking care of mail, garbage or plants, light cleaning, and, of course, all necessary animal care. "Pet Standard" plans include a generic check-up, expected animal care, and a brief trip outside for dogs or cats. These visits are usually 15-30 minutes long. It is expected that clients provide enough supplies necessary for their pets. If I must provide supplemental supplies, they will be complimentary unless their value exceeds $10. A $10 convenience fee will be charged for errands or an excessive need of supplemental supplies. Grooming services will be $8. This will include bathing, light trimming, and nail clipping. For my clients' convenience, I have laid out the following charges.

Charges in Brief

"Pet Plus" Visitation..*$12.00 per visit*
(Usually last an hour and includes a 30-minute dog walk or 30 minutes of playtime, light cleaning, all necessary animal care for one pet)

"Pet Standard" Visitation ....*$6.00 per visit*
(Usually lasts 15-30 minutes and includes a generic check-up, necessary animal care for one pet)

Overnight or extended pet visitation......................................*$30.00*

Grooming Services...*$8.00*
(Includes bathing, light trimming, nail clipping)

Each additional pet, includes all necessary care

Dogs...$6.00

Cats (indoor) $4.00

Cats (outdoor)...$3.00

Birds $3.00

Small mammals..$3.00

Rabbits...$4.00

Small reptiles $3.00

Larger reptiles...$4.00

*All fish care is free

Gourmet homemade treats

Dog biscuits or kitten cookies per half pound...........$3.00

Dog biscuits or kitten cookies per pound..................$5.00

Custom large dog birthday biscuit $5.00

Custom large kitten cake.....................................$5.00

*Convenience fee for errands or supplemental
supplies in excess*...$10.00

Pet Grooming Resources

N.D.G.A.A.
National Dog Groomers Assn. of America
Phone: 724-962-2711
Email: info@ndgaa.com
www.nationaldoggroomers.com

I.S.C.C.

International Society of Canine Cosmetologists

Phone: 877-738-4451

www.petstylist.com

I.P.G.

International Professional Groomers, Inc.

Phone: 1-503-551-2397

Info@ipgicmg.com

Ipgicmg.com

Other associations may be listed in the PetGroomer.com

Index

A

Advertising 7, 10, 32, 93, 97,
107, 117, 123

B

Bakery 8, 113
Biking 20, 40
Birds 6, 70, 74, 107, 115, 127,
138
Brand 5, 10, 30, 32, 36, 66, 126
Burnout 8, 49, 115, 116, 123

C

Checklist 6-8, 62, 63, 72, 83, 84,
86, 129
Client agreement 6, 51, 52, 58
Client interview 6, 20, 58, 82,
105
Cold calling 7, 97, 124

E

Emergencies 17, 20
Expansion 8, 111, 124, 135
Expenses 6, 39, 46, 55, 125

F

Facebook 7, 22, 38, 39, 48, 62,
99, 102, 105, 134, 136
Fish 6, 69, 71, 72, 75, 81, 84,
104, 129, 137, 138

G

Goal setting 35
Grooming 8, 23, 40, 42, 105,
107, 111, 112, 124, 132, 134,
136-138

H

Holiday 41, 83
Homemade Bird Balls 115
Homemade Dog Biscuits 114

I

Instagram 7, 38, 39, 99, 134, 136
Interview 6, 19, 20, 44, 57, 58,
     60, 62, 82, 105

K

Keys 20, 33, 34, 43, 58, 62-64,
     83, 86, 131, 133
Kitten Cookies 114, 138
Kittens19, 22, 125

L

Litter 23, 61, 63, 68, 69, 84, 87,
     130

M

Mammals 26, 70, 71, 73, 74, 138
Medication 14, 70

N

Nutrition26, 27

P

Profile 60, 63, 64, 90, 99, 102
Profit   42, 43, 48, 113, 126
Puppies 23, 25, 42

R

Record 18, 36, 45, 90
Reptiles 6, 73, 138

S

Schedule 19-21, 41, 43, 70, 75,
     77, 78, 86, 105, 108, 112, 115
Self-evaluation 35, 126
Service kit 6, 20, 64, 127
Social Media 5, 7, 22, 32, 34, 37,
     38, 48, 50, 97-99, 101-103,
     117, 132, 136
Suet 115, 127
Survey 46, 48, 81, 127

T

The Dog Whisperer 26
Transportation 6, 23, 39, 40, 42,
     54
Twitter , 38, 39, 62, 99, 134, 136

V

Veterinarian 7, 8, 53-55, 85, 86,
     127, 130, 131

W

Walking 1, 2, 20, 23, 40, 67, 94,
     102, 110, 134
WordPress 7, 101, 105, 134, 136

About the Author

Yvonne Bertovich is currently a journalism student at the University of Florida. She has offered pet-sitting services for friends and neighbors since she was nine years old. Growing up, Yvonne's only siblings were two large Labrador Retrievers named Rembrandt and Cami. She currently has a 12-year-old Lab named Cake who lives at her family's home in Tampa, Florida.

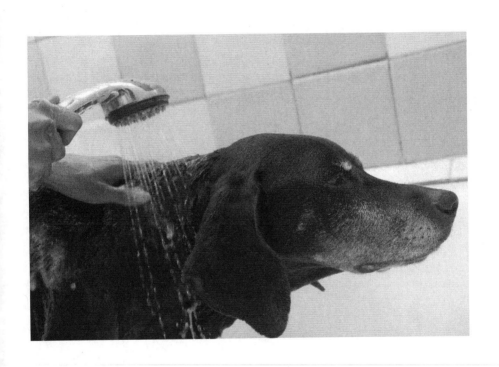

they are leaving the care of their loved ones up to you and welcoming you into their homes. If you do not properly meet the needs of a client, you may not only lose their business, but you may also put the livelihood of their pet in danger. That being said, if you do get hired, this means that someone sees potential in you to provide the important care that his or her pet needs!

Even though you may choose to enlist the help of a family member or friend to assist you, it is important that you are able to be self-sufficient, consistent, and dependable. It is also important that you are able to remain calm during emergencies, even though you hopefully won't encounter any. There is a lot of responsibility when you involve a person's home and their pet's safety.

Ask yourself:

- Are you able to make quick, wise decisions in difficult situations?

- Are you comfortable working alone in new environments or houses that may be strange to you?

- Can you care for an animal that is in distress without getting frustrated? Would you be able to handle a mean animal if you had to?

Even though becoming a pet-sitter will have you focused on the well-being and care of animals, your success is ultimately determined by your savvi-ness in business. If you're not feeling confident right now — fear not — you still have a whole book to read! Becoming business savvy does not mean transforming into some pinstripe-suited corporate cog. Basic business skills can be learned by anyone of any age.

One of the most important aspects of running a pet-sitting business will be record keeping. Whether you decide to use scheduling apps or reminders, there will probably be some important paperwork you should keep track of as well. This can include special instructions for certain pets under your care, client agreements or profiles, and even your checks or bank statements.

Bark Break!
Fake it till you make it

Yes, that's an obnoxious cliché segue — oh, gosh, and now it rhymes too. But it's the truth and can be applied to a wide variety of social and professional settings.

If you're not naturally the most confident cat in the room, pretend that you are. When you're representing your business or meeting with a client, visualize a 2.0 version of yourself and step into those symbolic shoes or put on that poetical coat. Stand up straight for goodness sake. Faking it can also refer to how old you are numerically versus the level of maturity you present yourself with. It can mean, in a loose sense, faking how much experience you have. If you come off incredibly knowledgeable and passionate, your customers may assume you've been pet-sitting since birth.

So we've covered the "faking it" part, what's the "making it" part? That's subjective to you. Maybe you're only in pet-sitting for the money (but that's doubtful). Maybe you're in it because you enjoy money, and you care about building relationships and bettering the lives of pets. Maybe you care about making a name for yourself. Yeah, that all sounds good.
